Black Historical Figures

INVENTORS

Copyright © 2022 by Every Dollar Countz LLC
All rights reserved. This book or any portion thereof
may not be reproduced or used in any manner whatsoever
without the express written permission of the publisher
except for the use of brief quotations in a book review.

TABLE OF CONTENTS

35 GEORGE W CARVER

107 LEWIS LATIMER

155 PATRICIA BATH

3 George Speck	67 Mark Dean	131 Elijah McCoy
11 Frederick Jones	75 Percy Julian	139 Alexander Miles
19 Garrett Morgan	83 Otis Boykin	147 Charles Drew
27 MarieVan Brown	91 Mary Kenner	155 Patricia Bath
35 George W Carver	99 Phillip Downing	163 Wallace Amos
43 Granville T Woods	107 Lewis Latimer	171 Majorie S. Joyner
51 Lonnie Johnson	115 Henry Sampson	179 Gerald Lawson
59 Lisa Gelobter	123 Madam C.J. Walker	187 Sarah Boone
		195 Lyda D. Newman

These Workbooks are geared to intrigue, inspire and motivate you to want to learn more about these Black Historical Figures(BHFs) and others. Also to do more research on your own. We know this isn't all the history of these individuals. We want you to do some of the research also. We try to be as accurate as possible during our research. If there are some stories or questions that aren't as stated, please contact us at info@wegonnalearntoday.com.

George Speck

George Speck

July 15, 1824 – July 22, 1914
CHEF

LEFT BLANK ON PURPOSE

George Speck

George Speck

George Speck

George Speck

George Speck

George Speck

Directions: read the bio below and answer the following questions.

Hi, my name is George Speck. I was born on July 15, 1824, in Saratoga County, NY. When I was in my mid-twenties, I was hired by Moon's Lake House, a high-end restaurant that catered to wealthy Manhattan families. I got my nickname while working here. Commodore Cornelius Vanderbilt, who was a shipping tycoon, was a regular customer and would often forget my name, so he would call me "Crum." I figured that "a crumb is bigger than a speck," so I decided to keep the nickname. In 1860, I opened my own restaurant, which was called Crum's. My cuisine was in high demand among Saratoga Springs' tourists and elites. I grew everything I could on my own small farm. George said, "the invention of Saratoga Chips was an accident. My sister Catherine Wicks had chipped off a piece of the potato which, by accident, fell into the pan of fat. Catherine fished it out with a fork and set it down upon a plate beside her on the table." I tasted it, thought it was good and started providing every table with a basket of chips.

1. What was the name of the restaurant I got my start at?
   A. Crum's
   B. Moon Lake House
   C. Knickerbocker Hall Restaurant
2. What year did I open Crum's?
   A. 1850
   B. 1855
   C. 1860
3. I'm known as the person who invented?
   A. Potato Chips
   B. Fine cuisine
   C. Fried wild duck

Directions: Answer the questions to solve the crossword puzzle. You can use the internet if you get stuck on any question.

Across

1) George's chips were initially known as potato ___ and also Saratoga chips.
4) In 1860, George started his own _____ called Crum's.
7) George used Crum, which is his father's last name as a _____.
8) At George's restaurant he served potato chips as an _____ at every table.

Down

2) George was the ____ of Cary Moon's Lake House.
3) George never ____ his potato chips and never tried to market them outside of his business.
5) George was a mixture of black American and ____ Indian.
6) George had ____ that would travel ten plus miles to try his potato chips in the mid 1800s.

Directions: Read and answer the questions. These are your opinions so the answers will vary.

Would you rather go camping or stay in a hotel? Why?

What's your favorite seasoning & why?

What career are you most interested in? Why?

Directions: Unscramble the words below about George. See if you can get the bonus word.

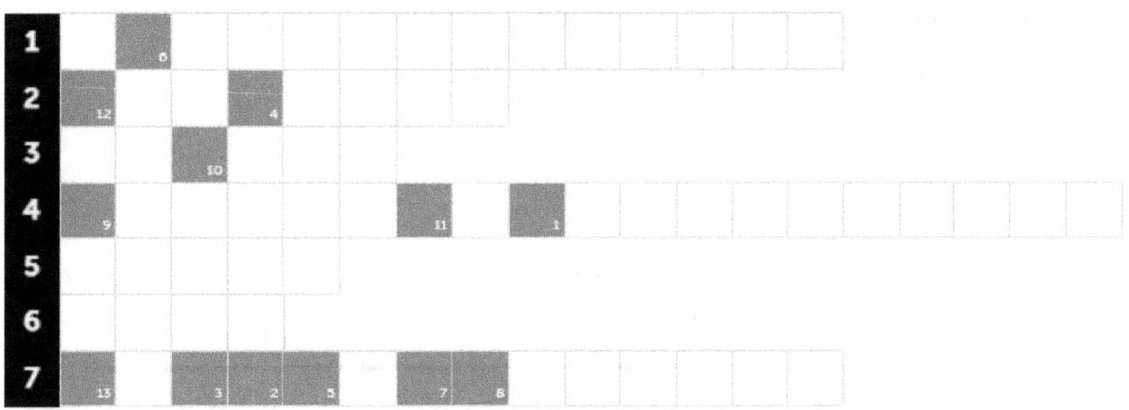

BONUS WORD

Unscramble Words

1) easmlusknoheoo   **2)** toatspoe   **3)** maokwh
4) tcoierneldsbvailurn   **5)** talma   **6)** hfec
7) gayctoaoatrnsu

Directions: This is the WGLT Challenge. Solve the cryptogram. As the puzzle solver, you need to find which number belongs to which character. And this can be pretty challenging! You will need to match the number with the letter. There are some letters given to you below. This will help you solve the other words and unlock more characters. **Good Luck.**

Frederick McKinley Jones

Frederick McKinley Jones

May 17, 1893 – February 21, 1961
ENGINEER

LEFT BLANK ON PURPOSE

Frederick McKinley Jones

Frederick McKinley Jones

Frederick McKinley Jones

Frederick McKinley Jones

Frederick McKinley Jones

Frederick McKinley Jones

Directions: read the bio below and answer the following questions.

Hi, my name is Frederick McKinley Jones. I was born on May 17, 1893, in Covington, KY. When I was 11, I started working odd jobs, one was cleaning a garage. By age 14, I was working as an automobile mechanic and eventually became the garage foreman. In 1912, I ended up in Hallock, Minnesota, where I did mechanical work on a farm. I was 20 when I got my engineering license. I served in the U.S. Army as an electrician during World War I. After the war, I came back to Hallock and ended up building a transmitter for the town's first radio station, as well as a device to combine sounds with motion pictures. In 1927, I was hired by Joseph A. Numero to be an electrical engineer. I was hired to help improve the audio equipment made by his firm. In 1938, I began designing the Thermo-Control Model A automatic truck refrigeration unit. These cooling units were especially important during World War II since they could be used to preserve blood, medicine and food for use at army hospitals and on open battlefields.

1. What did I start off doing?
    A. Engineer
    B. Electrician
    C. Automobile Mechanic
2. What year did I get hired as an Electrical Engineer?
    A. 1912
    B. 1927
    C. 1938
3. Which of my inventions helped the most in World War II?
    A. Cooling Units
    B. Movie-Ticket dispenser
    C. Portable X-ray machine

Directions: Find the words associated with Frederick's life and career.

G	P	G	L	O	R	E	B	B	W	E	G	M	O	Y	R	S
R	A	X	R	E	F	R	I	G	E	R	A	T	I	O	N	D
A	T	M	Q	E	P	H	O	B	A	Y	Z	X	E	B	N	W
W	E	W	O	U	L	M	W	S	W	Z	L	R	M	P	L	B
O	N	B	P	D	G	G	E	M	R	F	U	Q	C	C	P	K
R	T	O	I	L	E	H	T	C	N	E	G	S	P	O	L	A
L	S	X	C	N	Y	L	Z	T	N	N	E	Z	C	V	L	S
D	B	S	D	G	S	A	C	E	I	B	U	N	Z	I	B	H
W	P	B	Z	U	I	K	R	K	N	D	N	E	I	N	J	O
A	K	R	X	M	H	P	O	P	V	O	X	N	E	G	Q	Y
R	Z	R	G	V	E	M	F	F	E	Z	E	G	V	T	N	O
O	X	K	B	R	R	G	H	A	N	M	B	V	A	O	I	E
N	I	G	T	E	Z	B	N	S	T	F	R	N	Q	N	N	R
E	X	N	H	L	B	C	S	K	O	O	I	J	Y	E	B	I
X	E	T	I	T	A	X	D	G	R	Y	S	L	S	E	K	I
S	D	I	R	F	G	O	E	G	Z	D	L	F	E	B	I	A
W	W	Z	T	A	J	H	E	M	A	F	F	O	L	L	A	H

Find These Words

COVINGTON	INVENTOR	HALLOFFAME
ENTREPRENEUR	PATENTS	REFRIGERATION
ENGINEER	WORLDWARONE	THERMOKING
MODELC		

15

Directions: Read and answer the questions. These are your opinions so the answers will vary.

Would you rather ride a bike or a scooter?

What's your favorite website to visit?

Share a special memory you shared with family.

Directions: Read and answer the questions below. There are clues in the puzzle to help you. Try to solve the cryptic message.

Clue for cryptic message: Frederick was this since the age of twenty.

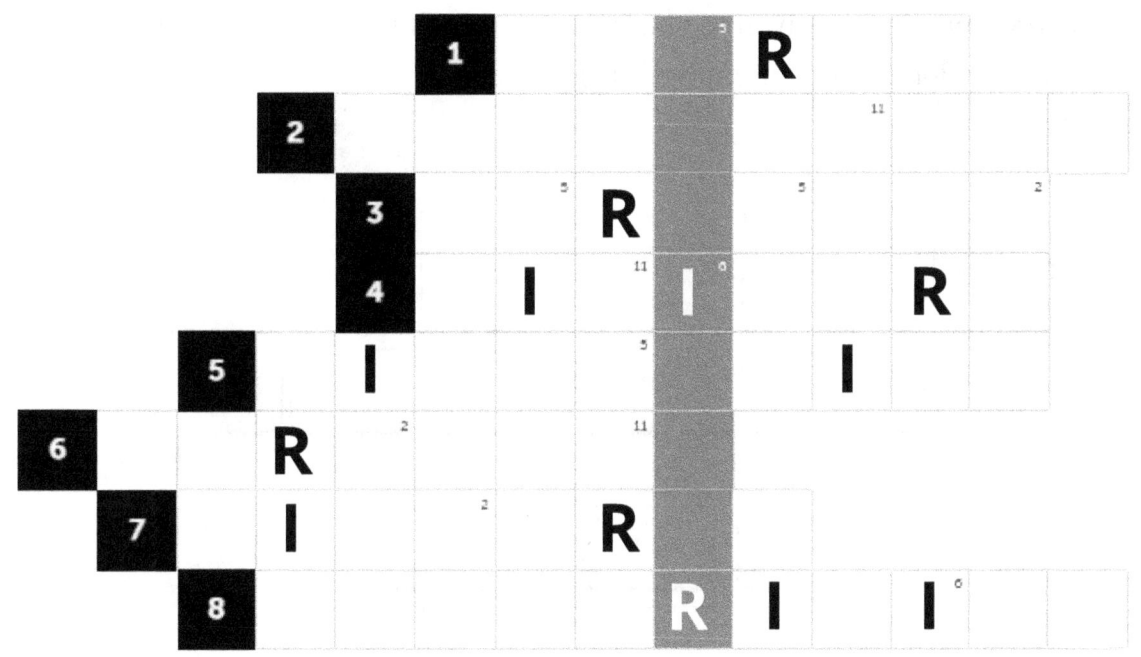

Questions

1) Frederick co-founded the U.S. ___ Control Company (later the Thermo King Corporation) in 1939.

2) Frederick was the winner of the National Medal of ____.

3) Frederick served as a ___ in World War I.

4) Frederick's Model C units were manufactured for ____ use during World War II, preserving blood, medicine and food.

5) Frederick patented a ticket ____ machine for movie theaters.

6) Frederick developed a _____ x-ray machine.

7) Frederick invented a device to combine sound with motion ___.

8) Frederick performed the wiring necessary to equip his camp with ___.

Directions: This is the WGLT Challenge. Solve the cryptogram. As the puzzle solver, you need to find which number belongs to which character. And this can be pretty challenging! You will need to match the number with the letter. There are some letters given to you below. This will help you solve the other words and unlock more characters. **Good Luck.**

A	B	C	D	E	F	G	H	I	J	K	L	M	N	O
20	22	21	3	2		5	10	13		1	26	25	18	23

P	Q	R	S	T	U	V	W	X	Y	Z
17		9	15	16	7	11			8	

13 16 10 13 18 1
I T H I N K

23 9 13 5 13 18 20 26   11 23 13 21 2 15
O R I G I N A L   V O I C E S

5 2 16   18 23 16 13 21 2 2 3.
G E T   N O T I C E E D.

22 7 16   25 23 15 16
B U T   M O S T

13 25 17 23 9 16 20 18 16 26 8 ,   13
I M P O R T A N T L Y ,   I

16 10 13 18 1   8 23 7
T H I N K   Y O U

15 10 23 7 26 3   10 20 11 2   20
S H O U L D   H A V E   A

15 16 23 9 8   16 23   16 2 26 26.
S T O R Y   T O   T E L L.

18

Garrett Morgan

March 4, 1877 – July 27, 1963
BUSINESSMAN

19

LEFT BLANK ON PURPOSE

Garrett Morgan

Garrett Morgan

Garrett Morgan

Garrett Morgan

Garrett Morgan

Garrett Morgan

Directions: read the bio below and answer the following questions.

Hi, my name is Garrett Augustus Morgan Sr. I was born on March 4, 1877, in Claysville, Bourbon County, KY. I reached the sixth grade at Branch Elementary School, but like many African American kids, I had to find work to help my family survive. In 1985, I began repairing sewing machines for a clothing manufacturer and got my first patent for an improved sewing machine. I also invented a zigzag attachment for sewing machines. In 1907, I opened my own repair business and a year later, me and my wife, Mary Anne, opened Morgan's Cut Rate Ladies Clothing Store. In 1914, I patented a breathing device that I called a "smoke hood" or "safety hood," which provided its wearers with a safer breathing experience in the presence of smoke, gases and other pollutants. In 1923, I created a new kind of traffic signal: it had a warning light that alerted drivers that they would need to stop.

1. What was considered my first invention?
    A. Improved sewing machine
    B. Zigzag attachment
    C. Breathing device
2. What year did I open my own business?
    A. 1908
    B. 1907
    C. 1906
3. Which invention did I enhance with my idea?
    A. Chemical hair-processing
    B. Smoke hood
    C. Traffic signal

Directions: Answer the questions, to solve the crossword puzzle. You can use the internet if you get stuck on any question.

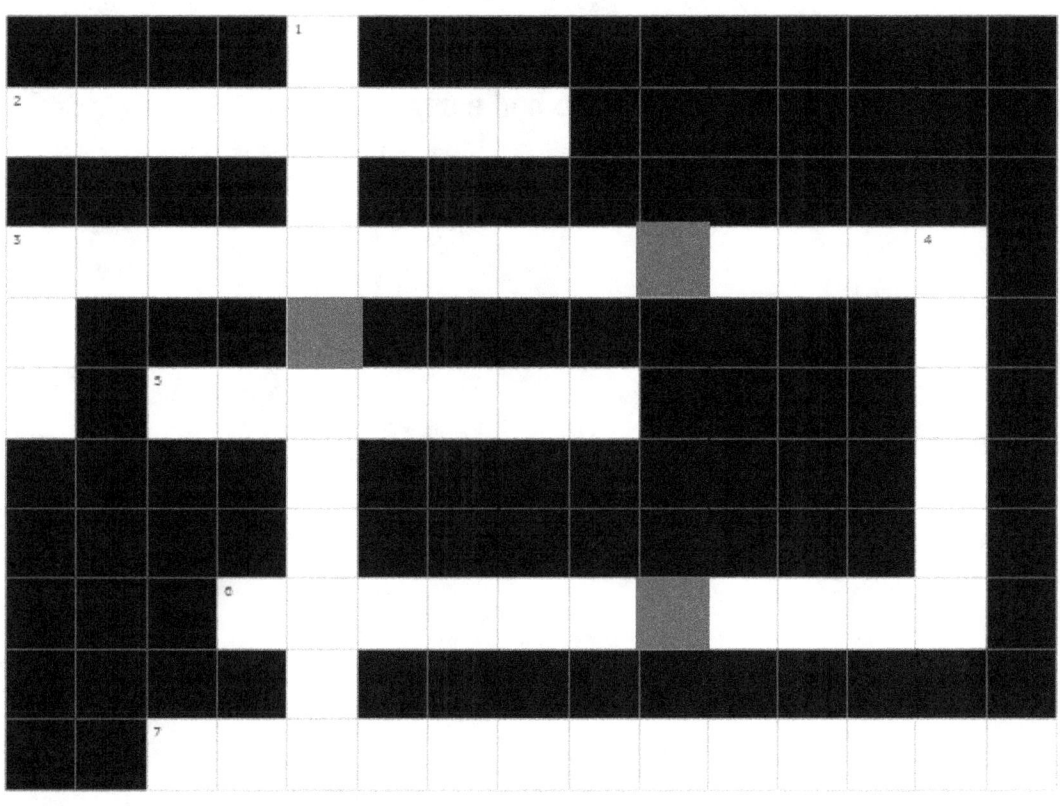

Across
2) Garrett began repairing sewing machines for a ____ manufacturer in Cleveland, OH..
3) Garrett launched the African American newspaper the _____.
5) In 1922, Garret filed for a patent for a traffic control device with a ____ position.
6) In 1914, Garrett patented a breathing device, or "_____," providing its wearers with a safer breathing experience in the presence of smoke, gases and other pollutants.
7) In 1910, Garrett invented a curved-tooth comb for hair ____.

Down
1) In 1907, Garrett opened his own sewing machine and _____ shop.
3) Garrett was the first African-American to own a ____ in Cleveland, OH.
4) Garrett made a ____ into a cream that straightens hair.

Directions: Read and answer the questions. These are your opinions so the answers will vary.

Would you rather stay up late or go to bed early?

What's your favorite movie?

Where do you hope to live someday?

Directions: Unscramble the words below about Garrett. See if you can get the bonus word.

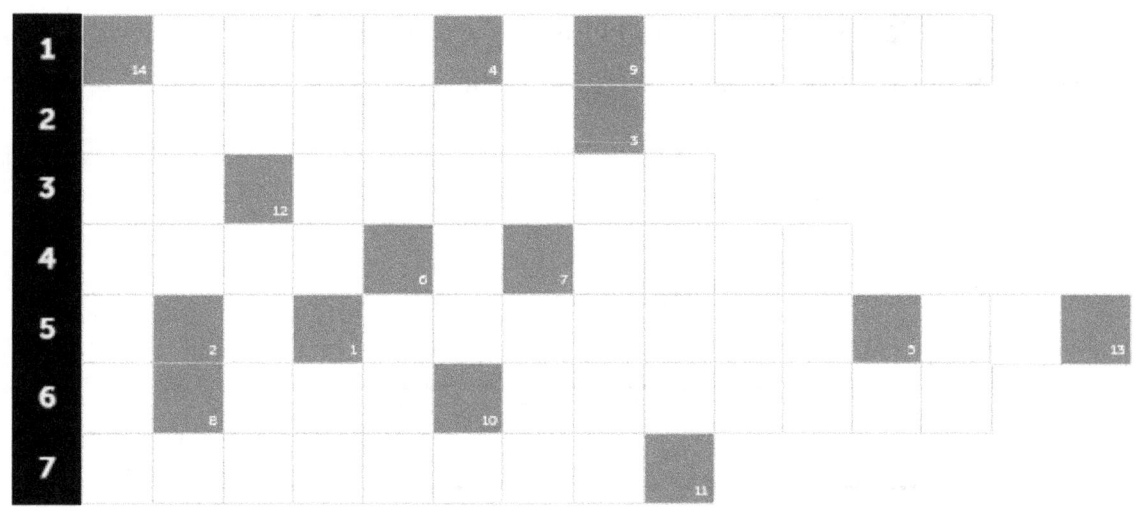

BONUS WORD

Unscramble Words

1) isncwehenmaig **2)** rontevin **3)** dnlcvaeel
4) isnueasmnsb **5)** emicantouyldmer **6)** fitgsfaarcnli
7) soeodmhko

Directions: This is the WGLT Challenge. Solve the cryptogram. As the puzzle solver, you need to find which number belongs to which character. And this can be pretty challenging! You will need to match the number with the letter. There are some letters given to you below. This will help you solve the other words and unlock more characters. **Good Luck.**

Marie Van Brittan Brown

Marie Van Brittan Brown

October 30, 1922 – February 2, 1999
INNOVATOR

27

LEFT BLANK ON PURPOSE

Marie Van Brittan Brown

Marie Van Brittan Brown

Marie Van Brittan Brown

Marie Van Brittan Brown

Marie Van Brittan Brown

Marie Van Brittan Brown

Directions: read the bio below and answer the following questions.

Hi, my name is Marie Van Brittan Brown. I was born on October 30, 1922, in Jamaica, Queens, NY. I worked as a nurse and my husband Albert Brown worked as an electrician. Albert worked late hours and we lived in a high-crime area. I didn't feel safe while he was at work, so we came up with a security system. The invention consisted of four peepholes, a sliding camera, TV monitors and microphones. The cameras could go from peephole to peephole. These cameras were connected to the TV monitors inside my home and using those TV monitors, I could see who was at the door without having to actually open the door. The microphone allowed me to talk with whoever was outside without opening the door. In 1966, we submitted a patent application for my invention. It was the first patent of its kind. The patent was granted by the government in 1969.

1. What was my profession before my invention?
   A. Electrician
   B. Nurse
   C. Security
2. What year did I get my patent for my invention?
   A. 1966
   B. 1969
   C. 1960
3. What did I invent to make me feel more safe?
   A. Door Lock
   B. Peep hole
   C. Security System

Directions: Find the words associated with Marie's life and career.

H	V	C	O	S	Y	O	Z	X	O	V	N	M	J	W	C	Y	S
Y	O	Q	C	J	S	H	K	P	F	S	S	S	J	M	L	X	L
I	P	M	N	R	G	K	E	B	Z	L	I	S	Q	I	O	I	I
N	U	T	E	U	T	L	S	N	J	N	A	F	H	C	S	Z	D
U	O	H	B	S	C	Y	G	T	V	L	O	D	U	R	E	N	I
F	N	K	A	W	E	C	A	E	I	J	M	R	H	O	D	K	N
L	O	V	X	E	X	C	N	E	D	C	B	V	F	P	-	A	G
Q	T	L	B	D	Z	T	U	U	L	C	Y	J	Z	H	C	T	-
F	T	M	Z	Y	I	U	I	R	R	P	Y	K	W	O	I	P	C
Z	U	L	W	O	T	S	P	M	I	S	Z	I	S	N	R	O	A
R	B	B	N	N	R	B	C	T	A	T	E	X	T	E	C	W	M
G	M	S	E	L	O	H	P	E	E	P	Y	P	V	S	U	T	E
F	R	T	A	P	L	S	R	W	A	G	E	S	A	K	I	I	R
V	A	E	T	F	J	E	Y	Z	N	Z	E	O	Y	Y	T	D	A
P	L	A	U	Q	O	F	U	V	C	H	H	X	X	S	-	T	M
C	A	Q	D	B	J	A	N	B	F	R	U	T	I	G	T	I	O
J	A	J	J	P	K	L	P	W	M	X	R	A	T	N	V	E	D
X	T	S	N	E	E	U	Q	-	A	C	I	A	M	A	J	R	M

Find These Words

NURSE JAMAICA-QUEENS HOMESECURITYSYSTEM
INVENTIONS CLOSED-CIRCUIT-TV PEEPHOLES
ALARMBUTTON SLIDING-CAMERA MICROPHONES
PATENT

Directions: Read and answer the questions. These are your opinions so the answers will vary.

Would you rather play video games or play outside?

What's your favorite vegetable? fruit?

Describe the most beautiful place you've ever been.

Directions: Read and answer the questions below. There are clues in the puzzle to help you. Try and solve the cryptic message.

Clue for cryptic message: Marie is considered to be one of these.

Questions

1) Marie is _____ with the invention of the first closed circuit television.

2) Marie got an award from the National _____ Committee for the invention of the home security system.

3) Marie was _____ to create security system because it would take a long period for the police to come.

4) Marie's invention was the basis for the two-way _____ and surveillance features of modern security.

5) Marie was 43 years old when she _____ her version of the home security system.

6) Marie's _____ has more than ten inventions.

7) Marie was the inventor of the first home security _____.

8) Marie's original design had three _____ placed on the front door at different height levels.

9) Marie's' patent has been referenced by _____ other inventors.

33

Directions: This is the WGLT Challenge. Solve the cryptogram. As the puzzle solver, you need to find which number belongs to which character. And this can be pretty challenging! You will need to match the number with the letter. There are some letters given to you below. This will help you solve the other words and unlock more characters. **Good Luck.**

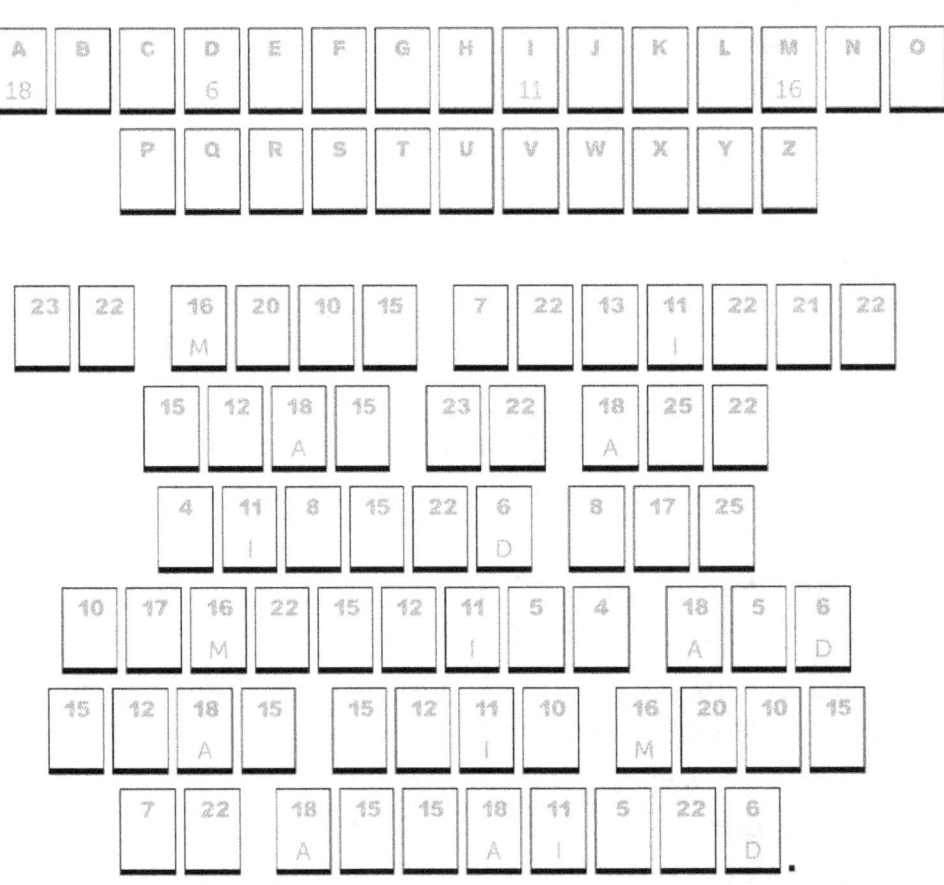

George Washington Carver

George Washington Carver

1864 – January 5, 1943
AGRICULTURAL SCIENTIST

LEFT BLANK ON PURPOSE

George Washington Carver

George Washington Carver

George Washington Carver

George Washington Carver

George Washington Carver

George Washington Carver

Directions: read the bio below and answer the following questions.

Hi, my name is George Washington Carver. I was born in 1864 in Diamond, MO. I graduated from Minneapolis High School. I earned my bachelor's degree and master's degree from Iowa State University. I was the first Black student there. I also taught as the first Black faculty member at Iowa State. In 1896, Booker T. Washington, the first principal and president of the Tuskegee Institute (which is now Tuskegee University), invited me to head its Agriculture Department. I taught there for 47 years. While there, I became a member of the Phi Beta Sigma fraternity. I developed techniques for improving soil that had been depleted by repeated plantings of cotton and came up with alternative crops to cotton and methods for preventing soil depletion. I developed hundreds of products using the peanut, the sweet potato and the soybean. Some of the products that I'm known for are roasted peanuts, peanut milk, Worcestershire sauce, cooking oils, salad oil, paper made from peanuts, cosmetics, soaps and wood stains.

1. Where did I get my Masters degree from?
    A. Highland University
    B. Iowa State University
    C. Simpson College
2. What fraternity am I a member of?
    A. Phi Beta Sigma
    B. Alpha Phi Alpha
    C. Omega Phi Psi
3. What product didn't I develop?
    A. Milk
    B. Peanut Butter
    C. Soap

Directions: Answer the questions, to solve the crossword puzzle. You can use the internet if you get stuck on any question.

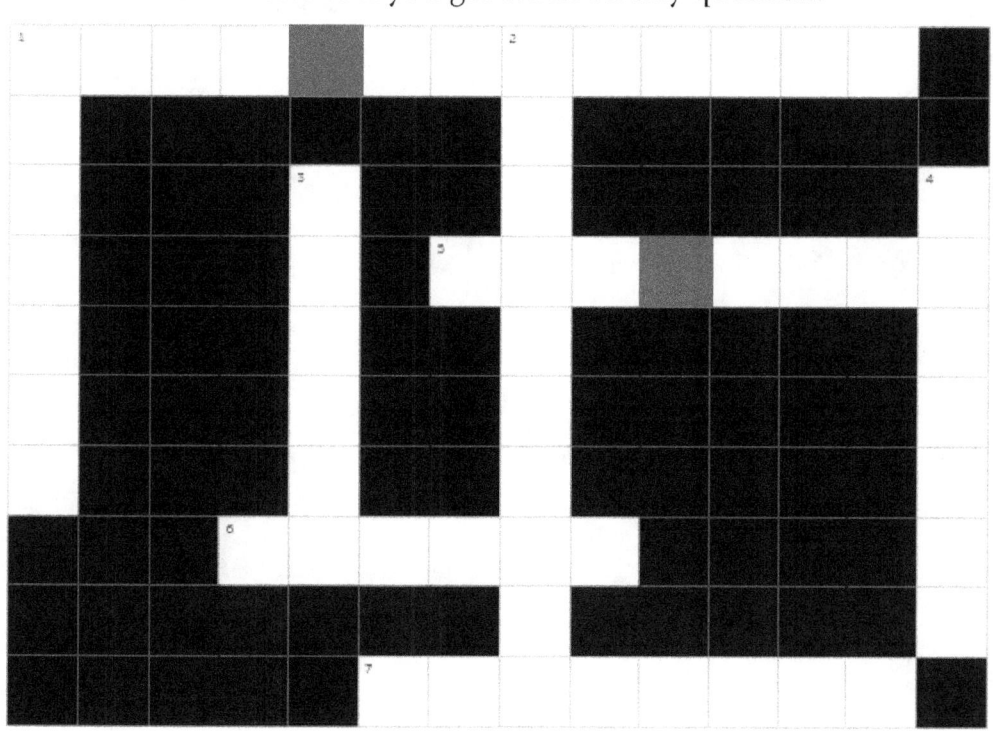

Across

1) George taught methods of _____, introduced several alternative cash crops for farmers that would also improve the soil of areas heavily cultivated in cotton.
5) George was a member of _____ Sigma fraternity.
6) George published a research bulletin, "How to Grow the _____ and 105 Ways of Preparing it For Human Consumption."
7) George was the Director of the Agriculture Department at _____ Normal and Industrial School.

Down

1) George helped Henry Ford make peanut rubber for _____ for World War II.
2) George developed _____ to improve soils depleted by repeated plantings of cotton.
3) George designed a ____ classroom to take education out to farmers called "Jesup wagon."
4) George only filed three _____ on the products he'd developed, so that they can be available to all people.

Directions: Read and answer the questions. These are your opinions so the answers will vary.

Would you rather get up early or sleep late?

What's your favorite activity to do at recess?

Share a special memory you had with a friend.

Directions: Unscramble the words below about George. See if you can get the bonus word.

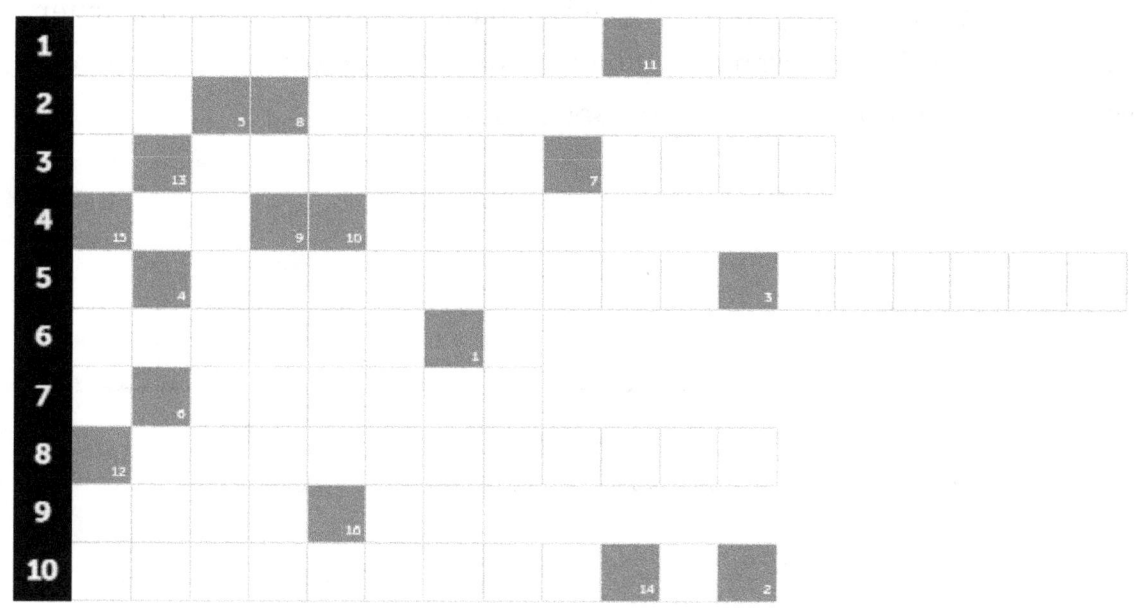

BONUS WORD

Unscramble Words

1) llpinoeidoset
2) emsfarr
3) kedoaolrnalbc
4) ttisscine
5) tiheynunhivigadsrl
6) utgeekse
7) absonsye
8) lartauugircl
9) umslgee
10) pacooirrntto

41

Directions: This is the WGLT Challenge. Solve the cryptogram. As the puzzle solver, you need to find which number belongs to which character. And this can be pretty challenging! You will need to match the number with the letter. There are some letters given to you below. This will help you solve the other words and unlock more characters. **Good Luck.**

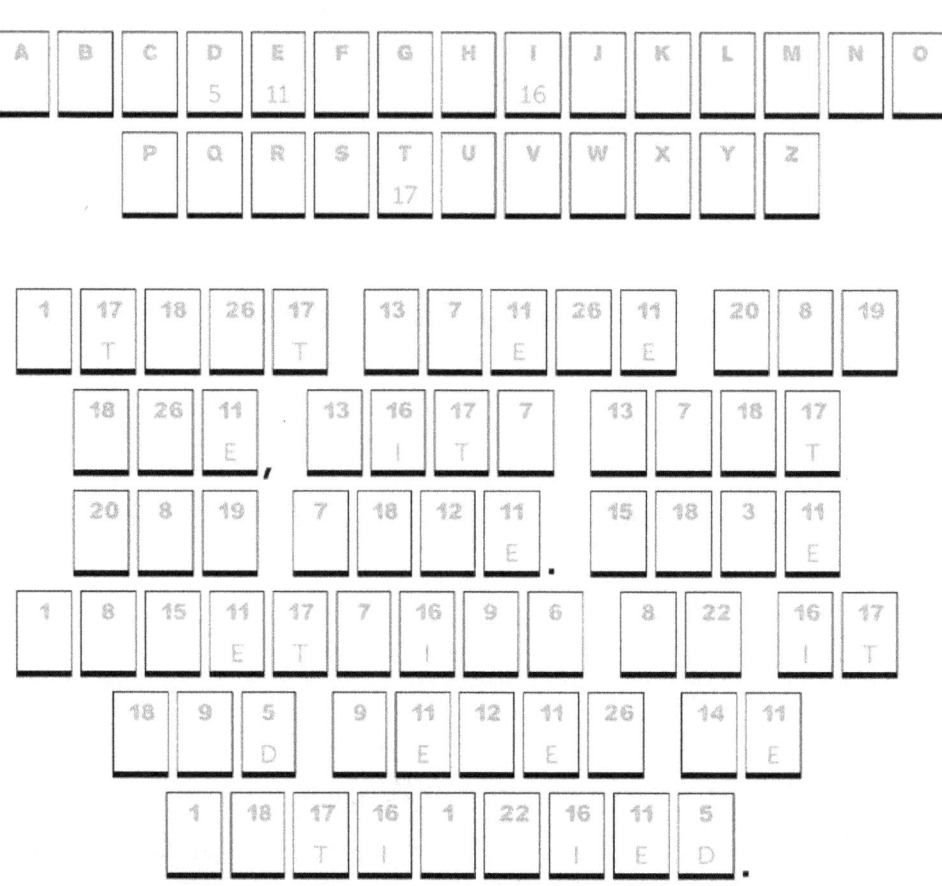

Granville T Woods

Granville T Woods

April 23, 1856 – January 30, 1910
MECHANICAL AND ELECTRICAL ENGINEER

LEFT BLANK ON PURPOSE

Granville T Woods

Granville T Woods

Granville T Woods

Granville T Woods

Granville T Woods

Granville T Woods

Directions: read the bio below and answer the following questions.

Hi, my name is Granville Tailer Woods. I was born on April 23, 1856, in Columbus, OH. I had to leave school when I was 10 to get a job to help my family. I got an apprenticeship in a machine shop and trained to be a machinist and blacksmith. In 1874, I worked at a rolling mill, the Springfield Iron Works. I studied mechanical and electrical engineering in college from 1876–1878. In 1878, I took a job aboard the steamer "Ironsides," and within two years, I became the chief engineer. In 1892, I moved my research operations to New York City. In 1884, I received my first patent for a steam boiler furnace and in 1885, I patented an apparatus that was a combination of a telephone and a telegraph. I called this device the "telegraphony". I sold the rights to this device to the American Bell Telephone Company. In 1887, I patented the Synchronous Multiplex Railway Telegraph, which allowed train stations and moving trains to communicate.

1. What was not one of the skills I learned when I was 10?
   A. Electrician
   B. Machinist
   C. Blacksmith
2. What year did I get my first patent?
   A. 1885
   B. 1884
   C. 1887
3. Which patent did I sell to American Bell?
   A. Telegraphony
   B. Steam boiler
   C. Synchronous Multiplex Railway Telegraph

Directions: Find the words associated with Granville's life and career.

M	I	D	A	I	R	B	R	A	K	E	Y	J	M	D	H	X	I
X	T	L	D	P	H	P	A	R	G	E	L	E	T	M	F	N	S
A	H	S	T	N	E	T	A	P	K	P	E	U	T	O	A	U	A
K	N	W	I	U	Q	F	J	M	I	B	E	A	M	V	M	L	F
C	A	D	B	X	W	I	P	W	B	G	B	F	W	Q	K	E	E
Z	N	E	D	N	E	R	P	Q	A	N	R	O	X	G	G	Z	T
K	Z	G	E	N	E	R	A	L	E	L	E	C	T	R	I	C	Y
P	C	M	C	D	B	H	F	P	M	Q	M	D	I	H	R	H	C
A	S	T	R	E	E	T	C	A	R	S	M	Y	N	P	G	N	I
L	P	D	M	B	T	I	X	B	H	Q	I	L	V	A	B	O	R
X	E	W	D	Y	D	M	I	J	K	M	D	S	E	R	F	R	C
I	Y	R	W	H	I	S	N	P	Y	D	Y	P	N	G	Z	V	U
K	J	Q	Y	D	M	K	Z	B	Z	V	T	V	T	O	Q	N	I
N	R	Q	Z	T	P	C	R	U	H	P	E	G	O	N	U	Q	T
V	M	J	Z	J	G	A	J	P	A	L	F	V	R	O	U	J	M
F	H	G	Z	A	Q	L	I	R	N	U	A	R	C	H	W	C	V
K	G	A	G	M	U	B	P	X	O	V	S	Q	D	P	O	Q	Y
W	D	I	W	I	S	C	M	Y	D	N	T	U	I	R	O	D	D

Find These Words

PATENTS
INVENTOR
PHONOGRAPH
AIRBRAKE

STREETCARS
SAFETYCIRCUIT
GENERALELECTRIC

BLACKSMITH
TELEGRAPH
SAFETYDIMMER

Directions: Read and answer the questions. These are your opinions so the answers will vary.

Would you rather ride a bike or a scooter?

What's your favorite book & why?

What are you most excited about doing when you are a teen then college student and then an adult?

Directions: Read and answer the questions below. There are clues in the puzzle to help you. Try and solve the cryptic message.

Clue for cryptic message: Granville worked to improve these.

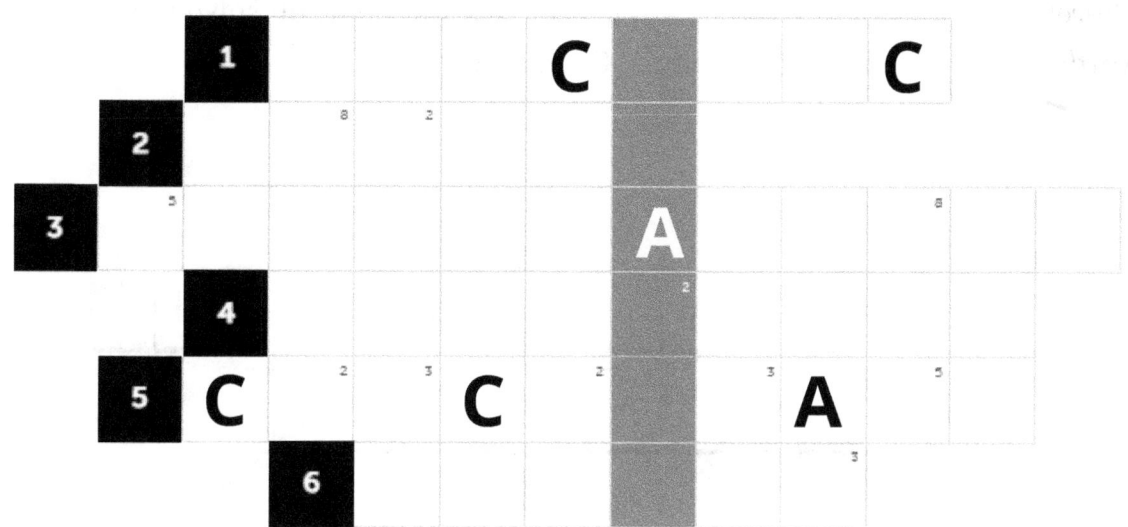

Questions

1) Granville invented and patented Tunnel Construction for the ___ railroad system.

2) Granville got his first patent for a steam ___ furnace in 1884.

3) Granville patented a device called "____", which allowed a telegraph station to send voice and telegraph messages through Morse code over a single wire.

4) Granville invented a device he called the Synchronous ____ Railway Telegraph.

5) Granville began the Woods Electric Company in _____, OH to market and sell his patents.

6) Granville nickname was "Black _____" because Thomas Edison tried to claim his telegraph system which he lost claim to in court twice.

Directions: This is the WGLT Challenge. Solve the cryptogram. As the puzzle solver, you need to find which number belongs to which character. And this can be pretty challenging! You will need to match the number with the letter. There are some letters given to you below. This will help you solve the other words and unlock more characters. **Good Luck.**

Lonnie Johnson

Lonnie Johnson

October 6, 1949 - PRESENT
AEROSPACE ENGINEER

LEFT BLANK ON PURPOSE

Lonnie Johnson

Lonnie Johnson

Lonnie Johnson

Lonnie Johnson

Lonnie Johnson

Lonnie Johnson

Directions: read the bio below and answer the following questions.

Hi, my name is Lonnie George Johnson. I was born on October 6, 1949, in Mobile, AL. I graduated from Williamson High School. I got my bachelor's degree in mechanical engineering and a master's degree in nuclear engineering from Tuskegee University. I worked on the stealth bomber program at the U.S. Air Force. In 1979, I went to work for NASA on a few projects, such as developing the nuclear power source for the Galileo mission to Jupiter. I was also an engineer on the Mariner Mark II Spacecraft series for the Comet Rendezvous and Saturn Orbiter Probe missions. In 1982, I began working with the Air Force. I designed and built plexiglass pieces for a water gun on the lathe in my basement. My daughter was my tester and the prototype was a success. My first order was for 1,000 guns. I couldn't handle that alone, so I looked for a partner. In 1991, Hasbro, who bought Larami and I changed the name from the "Power Drencher" to the "Super Soaker," and over two million units sold that summer.

1. What college did I get my Masters degree from?
    A. University of Alabama
    B. Tuskegee University
    C. Fisk University
2. Who did I go to work for in 1979?
    A. U.S. Airforce
    B. NASA
    C. Tuskegee University
3. In 1991 I partnered with Hasbro to sell?
    A. Nerf Gun
    B. Super Soaker
    C. Toy Robots

Directions: Answer the questions, to solve the crossword puzzle. You can use the internet if you get stuck on any question.

Across

2) Lonnie invented the Super Soaker water gun which is approaching sales of $1 _____.
4) Lonnie's Super Soaker was inducted into the National ___ Hall of Fame.
5) Lonnie got his ____ from George Washington Carver.
7) Lonnie was inducted into the State of Alabama ____ Hall of Fame
8) Lonnie won first place at a ___ in Alabama while in high school.

Down

1) Lonnie got an ____ Ph. D. in Science from Tuskegee University.
3) Lonnie worked for the U.S. Air Force, on the stealth ___ program.
6) Lonnie helped with developing the ____ power source for the Galileo mission to Jupiter.

Directions: Read and answer the questions. These are your opinions so the answers will vary.

Would you rather be a wizard or a superhero?

What's your favorite ice cream flavor?

Share a time when someone was extra kind to you.

Directions: Unscramble the words below about Lonnie. See if you can get the bonus word.

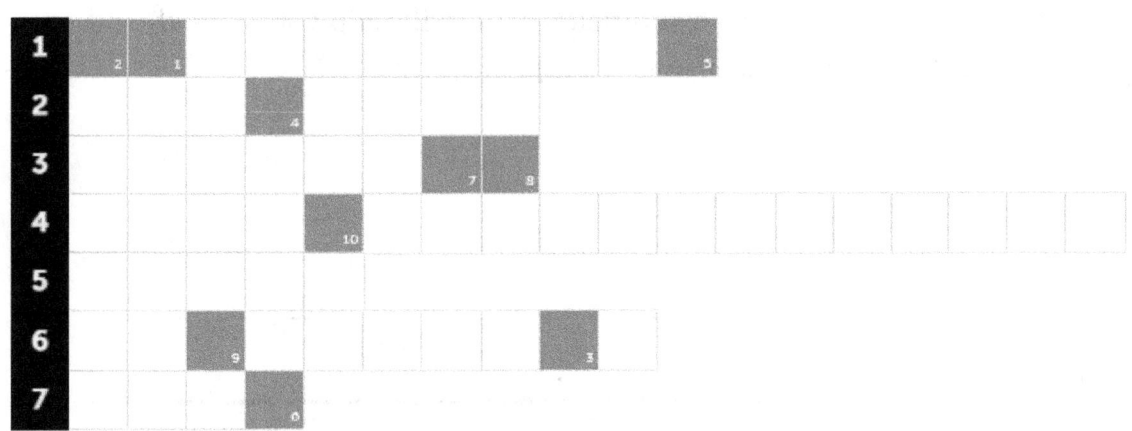

BONUS WORD

| 1 | 2 | 3 | 4 | 5 | 6 | 7 | 8 | 9 | 10 |

Unscramble Words

1) rsuaerspkeo 2) nrneigee 3) tniroevn
4) tuentekyreiiugsves 5) lxien 6) lihcecnmaa
7) frne

57

Directions: This is the WGLT Challenge. Solve the cryptogram. As the puzzle solver, you need to find which number belongs to which character. And this can be pretty challenging! You will need to match the number with the letter. There are some letters given to you below. This will help you solve the other words and unlock more characters. **Good Luck.**

A	B	C	D	E	F	G	H	I	J	K	L	M	N	O
8											26			15

P	Q	R	S	T	U	V	W	X	Y	Z
		5								

25 3 5 6 3 10 3 5 3 .
      R   R

21 12 8 21 ' 6 2 12 8 21 9
        A   A

8 26 2 8 16 6   6 8 16 21 15
A L   A   A   O

25 3 15 25 26 3 .   21 12 3 5 3 6 '
      O   L   R

7 15 3 8 16   5 15 22 21 3 .
   O   A   R   O

Lisa Gelobter

Lisa Gelobter

1971 – PRESENT
COMPUTER SCIENTIST

59

LEFT BLANK ON PURPOSE

Lisa Gelobter

Lisa Gelobter

Lisa Gelobter

Lisa Gelobter

Lisa Gelobter

Lisa Gelobter

Directions: read the bio below and answer the following questions.

Hi, my name is Lisa Gelobter. I was born in 1971 and I grew up in New York. I graduated with a bachelor's degree in computer science from Brown University. It took me 24 years to get my bachelor's degree. I finished in 2011. In 1995, I worked as the director of Program Management for Macromedia while still taking classes at college. I invented an animation software program that was later used to create the GIF, which is an animated image file that is used in texting and on social media. In 2007, I was a part of the launch team for Hulu. In 2010, I was the interim chief digital officer, head of digital product and Engineering G Operations for Black Entertainment Television (BET). In 2015, I became the chief digital service officer of the U.S. Department of Education for The White House under President Barack Obama. In 2017, I founded tEQuitable, which is a platform that is a confidential sounding board for employees that allows them to address issues of bias, discrimination and harassment. Companies can use it to make their workplaces more inclusive.

1. Where did I get my Bachelors degree from?
    A. New York University
    B. New York City College of Technology
    C. Brown University
2. What job allowed me to invent software to create GIFs?
    A. BET
    B. Macromedia
    C. The White House
3. What is the name of the company I founded?
    A. The FeedRoom
    B. tEQuitable
    C. Taligent

Directions: Find the words associated with Lisa's life and career.

A	M	C	P	F	P	Q	K	Z	U	L	C	Q	I	C	E	K	A	T
E	N	H	T	E	V	I	T	U	C	E	X	E	F	E	I	H	C	F
Q	N	I	Q	E	A	R	O	P	Y	P	N	M	K	H	R	P	K	V
S	Y	E	M	Y	T	I	S	R	E	V	I	N	U	N	W	O	R	B
P	W	F	X	A	X	L	V	L	W	H	B	V	W	E	U	U	E	Z
Z	R	D	Y	X	T	A	F	K	K	T	H	A	D	C	V	L	S	Y
B	X	I	X	Z	I	I	G	I	F	T	U	C	H	N	B	Z	K	S
G	E	G	A	J	Z	B	O	M	T	C	L	L	C	E	F	N	R	Y
K	P	I	X	Z	D	K	B	N	P	U	U	S	E	I	J	A	O	O
V	H	T	H	Y	H	R	P	M	S	E	H	E	S	C	Q	R	W	R
N	S	A	K	I	T	S	K	Y	B	O	S	L	X	S	R	W	T	F
S	V	L	M	X	G	I	G	Q	C	Q	X	B	W	R	R	R	E	B
G	S	O	K	G	E	O	P	K	H	P	L	A	D	E	I	Z	N	S
U	W	F	E	E	M	V	W	Q	A	U	X	T	S	T	G	F	T	G
S	S	F	W	O	K	A	I	L	D	W	O	I	O	U	O	W	E	M
G	S	I	Z	M	V	M	O	T	K	P	H	U	F	P	E	W	B	I
Y	M	C	A	E	I	Q	J	U	C	L	Z	Q	W	M	J	E	F	E
N	X	E	S	W	M	X	N	S	P	A	E	E	U	O	R	X	W	D
U	V	R	X	V	S	I	W	M	X	X	B	T	P	C	G	M	Y	Q

Find These Words

COMPUTERSCIENCE BETNETWORKS HULU
SHOCKWAVE BROWNUNIVERSITY TEQUITABLE
CHIEFEXECUTIVE ACTIVEX ANIMATIONS
CHIEFDIGITALOFFICER

Directions: Read and answer the questions. These are your opinions so the answers will vary.

Would you rather work in a group or work alone?

What's your favorite hobby or after school activity?

Where do you want to go to college?

Directions: Read and answer the questions below. There are clues in the puzzle to help you. Try and solve the cryptic message.

Clue for cryptic message: Lisa worked for this President.

Questions

1) Lisa is the _____ of tEQuitable.
2) Lisa was a member of the New York ____ League STEM Advisory Board.
3) Lisa was the Chief _____ Officer for BET Networks.
4) Lisa was ____ in the creation of Shockwave.
5) Lisa led the team that built the United States Department of ____ College Scorecard.

Directions: This is the WGLT Challenge. Solve the cryptogram. As the puzzle solver, you need to find which number belongs to which character. And this can be pretty challenging! You will need to match the number with the letter. There are some letters given to you below. This will help you solve the other words and unlock more characters. **Good Luck.**

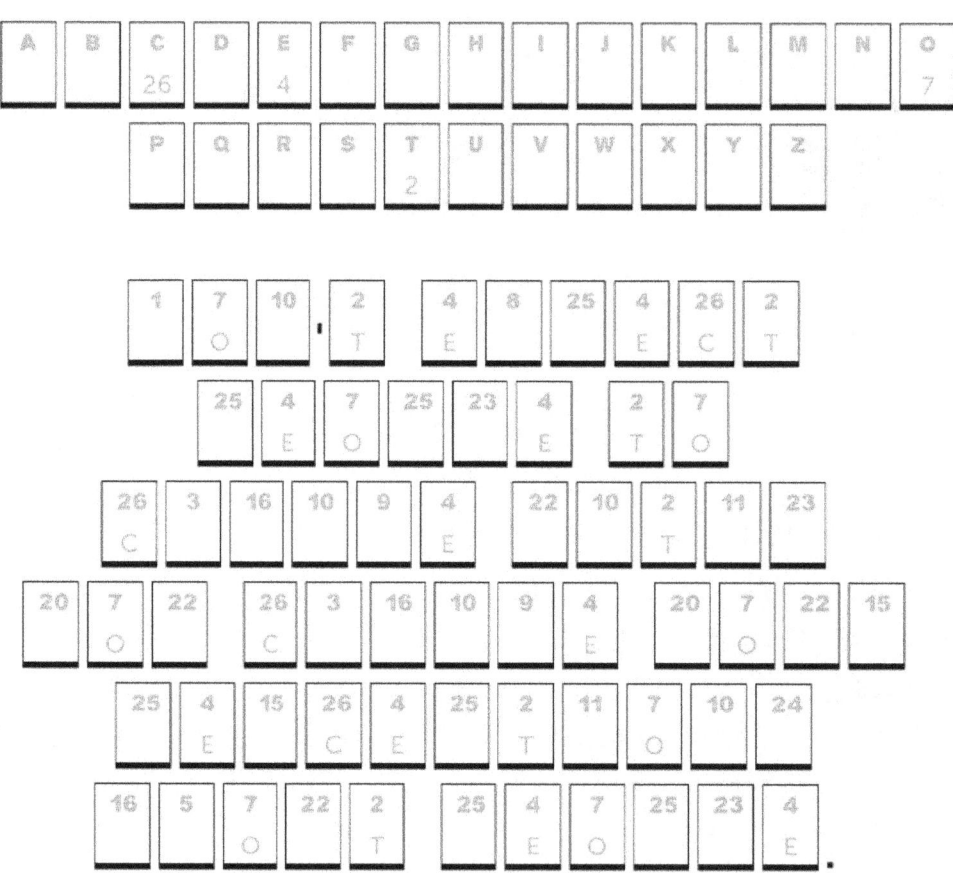

**March 2, 1957 – PRESENT
COMPUTER ENGINEER**

67

LEFT BLANK ON PURPOSE

Mark Dean

Mark Dean

Mark Dean

Mark Dean

Mark Dean

Mark Dean

Directions: read the bio below and answer the following questions.

Hi, my name is Mark E. Dean. I was born on March 2, 1957, in Jefferson City, TN. I graduated from Jefferson City High School. I received my bachelor's degree in electrical engineering from the University of Tennessee and my master's in electrical engineering from Florida Atlantic University. I got my doctorate in electrical engineering from Stanford University. I started working for IBM as an engineer. While working closely with my colleague, Dennis Moeller, I developed the new Industry Standard Architecture (ISA) systems bus, which was a new system that allowed peripheral devices such as disk drives, printers and monitors to be plugged directly into computers. This system made many processes more efficient and better integrated. My work also led to the development of the color PC monitor. I also led a team of engineers at the IBM labs in creating the first gigahertz chip. The chip can perform a billion calculations in a second.

1. What college did I get my Masters degree from?
    A. Stanford University
    B. University of Tennessee
    C. Florida Atlantic University
2. What company did I work for?
    A. IBM
    B. Apple
    C. Microsoft
3. Which invention is not mine?
    A. ISA systems bus
    B. Personal Computer
    C. Gigahertz chip

Directions: Answer the questions, to solve the crossword puzzle. You can use the internet if you get stuck on any question.

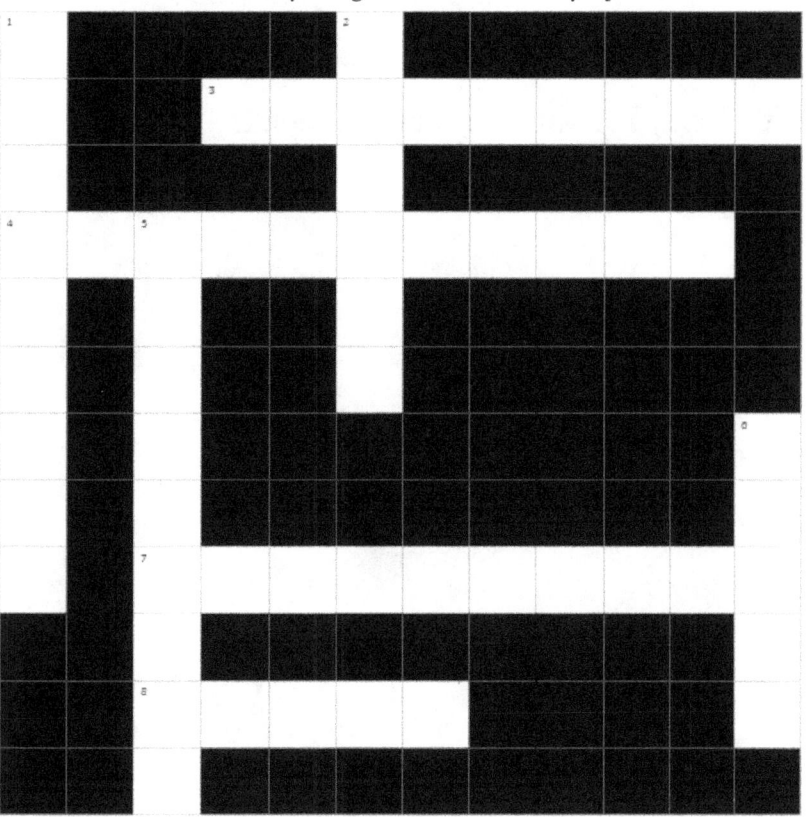

Across

3) Mark serves at Department of Electrical Engineering and Computer Science as the John Fisher Distinguished _____.
4) Mark was elected to the National Academy of _____.
7) Mark attended Florida Atlantic University where he got a master's degree in _____ engineering.
8) Mark owns _____ patent out of IBM's nine original patents and has over twenty patents.

Down

1) Mark was inducted at National _____ Hall of Fame due to his greatest inventions in technology.
2) Mark was part of the team that developed the industry standard architecture (ISA) systems bus that enables multiple devices, such as _____ and printers, to be connected to personal computers.
5) Mark led the team of engineers that created the first _____ chip at IBM.
6) Mark led the team that developed ___ PC monitor.

Directions: Read and answer the questions. These are your opinions so the answers will vary.

Would you rather play hide-and-seek or dodgeball?

What's your favorite video game?

Share about a time you learned an important life lesson.

Directions: Unscramble the words below about Mark. See if you can get the bonus word.

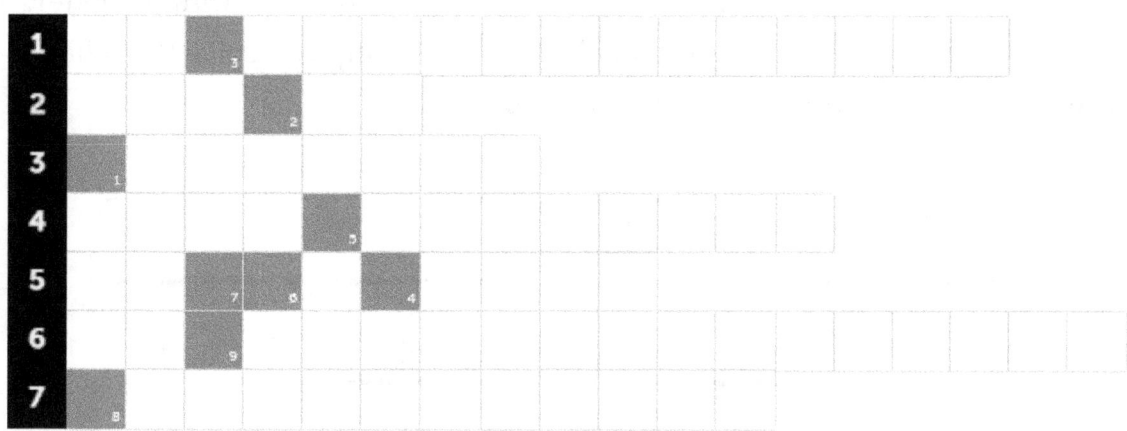

BONUS WORD

Unscramble Words
1) teuerrogceipenmn 2) sbuSAI 3) nnoivrte
4) iohrrsscpcepo 5) fmollaafhe 6) wsdrtnerwnproledoa
7) egtronaihzge

Directions: This is the WGLT Challenge. Solve the cryptogram. As the puzzle solver, you need to find which number belongs to which character. And this can be pretty challenging! You will need to match the number with the letter. There are some letters given to you below. This will help you solve the other words and unlock more characters. **Good Luck.**

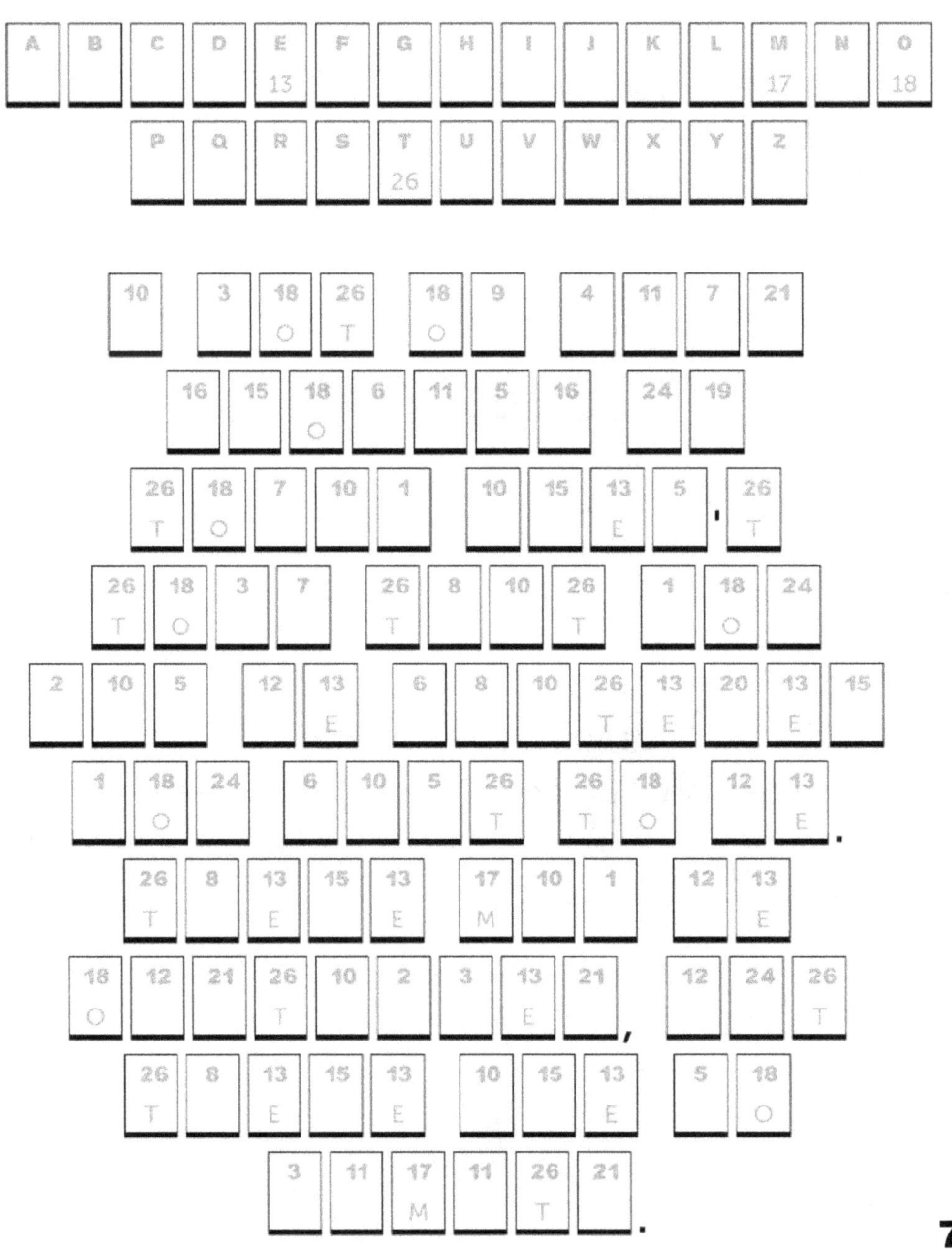

Percy Lavon Julian

Percy Lavon Julian

April 11, 1899 – April 19, 1975
CHEMIST

LEFT BLANK ON PURPOSE

Percy Lavon Julian

Percy Lavon Julian

Percy Lavon Julian

Percy Lavon Julian

Percy Lavon Julian

Percy Lavon Julian

Directions: read the bio below and answer the following questions.

Hi, my name is Percy Lavon Julian. I was born on April 11, 1899, in Montgomery, AL. I graduated from DePauw University as a valedictorian. I also became a member of the Phi Beta Kappa honor society. I received my master's degree from Harvard University. I ended up going to the University of Vienna for my Ph.D. in chemistry because Harvard worried that white students would resent being taught by an African American and they withdrew my teaching assistantship. While I was going to school, some of my work led me to discover the chemical synthesis of medicinal drugs from plants. I was the first person to synthesize the natural product physostigmine and was a pioneer in the industrial large-scale chemical synthesis of the human hormones progesterone and testosterone from plant sterols such as stigmasterol and sitosterol. Some of the other medications that the medical field has been able to create due to this discovery include cortisone, other corticosteroids and birth control pills, as well as medication for treating glaucoma and arthritis.

1. What college did I get my Ph. D from?
    A. DePauw University
    B. University of Vienna
    C. Harvard University
2. What honor society do I belong to?
    A. Phi Kappa Phi
    B. Gamma Beta Phi
    C. Phi Beta Kappa
3. Chemical synthesis of medicinal drugs helps treat?
    A. Arthritis
    B. Open wounds
    C. Headache

Directions: Find the words associated with Percy's life and career.

```
C H E M I C A L S Y N T H E S I S W
C B G L S F A D W Y R Y Z I S Q P X
H Z V E S F V L C Q U G A Z W Y L B
T Z G B I R T H C O N T R O L O A G
S G C G D I N N J Z T O U H W W N L
M T C C R O U O Y O K A T S J T A
Q L A R V Y X X N D X L R Q M J S U
J C O R T I S O N E O A D T X I T C
E D L R F O L A Y R W E Y F Z J E O
C R G S E J G I E D P M Y M W Q R M
B P A D N Y R T L H N R S W Z T O A
V F A F U F S R E Z T H O T V P L D
Z M X I I A O R M S V Z Y W U I S O
N V M L M W H G I U H I B A D L C M
Z K D I B A C M R W E T E T G T G C
A P T I N V E N T O R J A G U P U J
N S S Q S H R D E A B L N F S H B G
X D S A C N B F F X D T I P V T F W
```

Find These Words

WORLDWARTWO INVENTOR SOYBEAN
CHEMISTRY CORTISONE CHEMICALSYNTHESIS
STIMASTEROL PLANTSTEROLS BIRTHCONTROL
GLAUCOMA

79

Directions: Read and answer the questions. These are your opinions so the answers will vary.

Would you rather have indoor or outdoor recess?

What's your favorite board or card game?

What do you think you might be doing in 10 years?

Directions: Read and answer the questions below. There are clues in the puzzle to help you. Try and solve the cryptic message.

Clue for cryptic message: Percy created this from a soybean.

Questions

1) Percy created synthetic ___, a rare compound that helped relieve the crippling symptoms of rheumatoid arthritis.
2) Percy was a member of Phi ___ Kappa fraternity.
3) Percy founded Julian Associates and Julian ___ Institute.
4) Percy started his own company, Julian ___, out of Chicago.
5) Percy was named ___ of the Year by the city of Chicago.
6) Percy was a chemistry professor at ___ University.
7) Percy was the first African-American chemist ___ into the National Academy of Sciences.

81

Directions: This is the WGLT Challenge. Solve the cryptogram. As the puzzle solver, you need to find which number belongs to which character. And this can be pretty challenging! You will need to match the number with the letter. There are some letters given to you below. This will help you solve the other words and unlock more characters. **Good Luck.**

Otis Boykin

Otis Boykin

August 29, 1920 – March 26, 1982
ENGINEER

83

LEFT BLANK ON PURPOSE

Otis Boykin

Otis Boykin

Otis Boykin

Otis Boykin

Otis Boykin

Otis Boykin

Directions: read the bio below and answer the following questions.

Hi, my name is Otis Boykin. I was born on August 29, 1920, in Dallas, TX. I graduated from Booker T. Washington High School and was the valedictorian. I got my bachelor's degree from Fisk University. I moved to Chicago and worked a few jobs. By 1944, I was working for P.J. Nilsen Research Labs. In 1946, I started my own company, Boykin-Fruth, Inc., where I started working on different inventions. I received my first patent in 1959. I developed the wire precision resistor, which enabled manufacturers to accurately designate a value of resistance for an individual piece of wire in electronic equipment. Two years later, in 1961, I got a patent for an improved version of this concept, which was an inexpensive and easily producible electrical resistor model that could "withstand extreme accelerations and shocks and great temperature changes without change or breakage of the fine resistance wire or other detrimental effects." This invention has been used in guided missiles, televisions, pacemakers and IBM computers.

1. What HBCU did I go to?
    A. Clark University
    B. Fisk University
    C. Morehouse College
2. What year did I get my first patent?
    A. 1959
    B. 1961
    C. 1946
3. Electrical resistors aren't used in?
    A. Guided missiles
    B. Pacemakers
    C. Watch

Directions: Answer the questions, to solve the crossword puzzle. You can use the internet if you get stuck on any question.

Across

2) Otis invented a control unit for the artificial cardiac _____.
4) Otis invented an electronic control device in _____.
5) Otis opened an electronics research lab in ___ and Chicago.
6) Otis worked as a laboratory assistant for the _____ Radio and Television Corporation.
7) Otis attended Booker T. Washington High School where he was the _____.

Down

1) Otis helped improve wire resistor, which had reduced inductance and reactance, due to the ___ arrangement of the wire.
2) Otis held more than twenty-five _____ in his lifetime.
3) Otis invented a wire precision _____ used in radios and televisions.

Directions: Read and answer the questions. These are your opinions so the answers will vary.

Would you rather go to a zoo or an aquarium?

What's your favorite snack to eat?

Describe the most amazing thing you've ever seen in real life.

Directions: Unscramble the words below about Otis. See if you can get the bonus word.

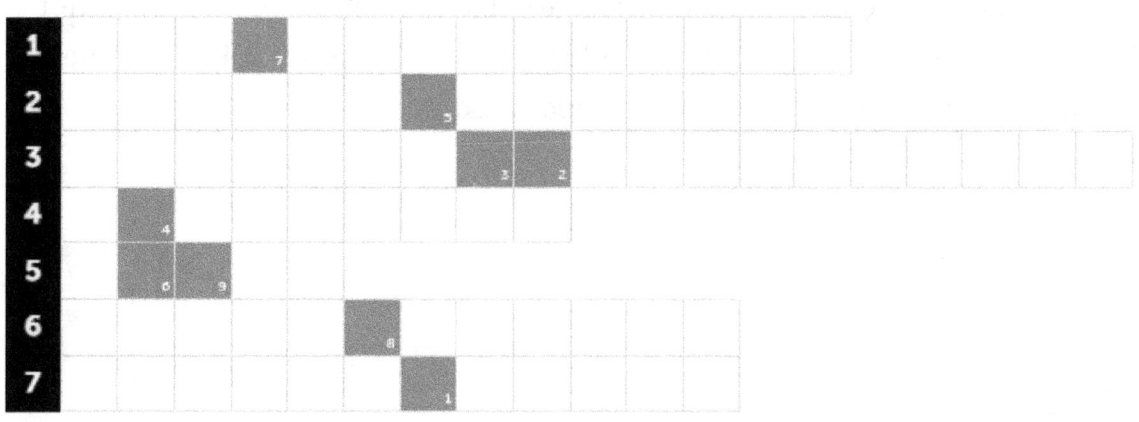

BONUS WORD

Unscramble Words

1) kuvifteyinsrsi **2)** uismesidgidle **3)** stciierallseorresct
4) reoascpea **5)** sprai **6)** reortswsriie
7) sormmcpbtuie

Directions: This is the WGLT Challenge. Solve the cryptogram. As the puzzle solver, you need to find which number belongs to which character. And this can be pretty challenging! You will need to match the number with the letter. There are some letters given to you below. This will help you solve the other words and unlock more characters. **Good Luck.**

Mary Kenner

Mary Kenner

May 17, 1912 - January 13, 2006
INVENTOR

LEFT BLANK ON PURPOSE

Mary Kenner

Mary Kenner

Mary Kenner

Mary Kenner

Mary Kenner

Mary Kenner

Directions: read the bio below and answer the following questions.

Hi, my name is Mary Beatrice Davidson Kenner. I was born on May 17, 1912, in Monroe, NC. I came from a family of inventors. My father and grandfather were also inventors, so it's no surprise that I became one as well. I even attempted to invent a self-oiling hinge for doors at six years old. I graduated from Dunbar High School. I attended Howard University, but I dropped out due to gender discrimination and financial difficulties. I became a professional florist in 1950 and ran my own flower shop into the 1970s while inventing in my spare time. I received my first patent in 1957 for the sanitary belt, which was the predecessor of adhesive pads and this invention was much more effective than the rags that women were using at the time. In 1976, I patented an attachment for a walker or wheelchair that included a hard-surfaced tray and a soft pocket for carrying items. I hold the record for the most patents held by any African American woman.

1. How old was I when I created my first invention?
   A. 12
   B. 6
   C. 20
2. What year did I get my first patent?
   A. 1958
   B. 1957
   C. 1976
3. I hold the record for the most ___ of any African American woman?
   A. Patents
   B. Jumping rope
   C. Typing words

94

Directions: Find the words associated with Mary's life and career.

T	C	T	Z	B	A	C	K	W	A	S	H	E	R	N	W	S	Q
O	L	T	R	T	K	P	F	P	N	E	O	F	C	D	Q	S	H
I	O	G	S	M	W	A	T	S	G	X	K	J	G	H	A	O	L
L	D	X	T	B	F	T	Z	R	F	D	T	Y	S	N	W	K	M
E	U	D	H	O	V	E	A	E	L	F	O	T	I	A	C	L	F
T	X	R	C	T	Y	N	B	W	V	R	O	T	R	A	E	R	S
P	D	Z	J	C	D	T	V	O	K	T	A	D	P	S	Y	S	Z
A	Q	L	D	U	S	S	F	L	W	R	U	-	F	R	H	G	R
P	G	Y	H	E	Q	J	C	F	Y	N	P	N	F	R	B	X	U
E	T	A	U	X	H	U	E	B	I	A	H	J	J	E	R	T	B
R	T	M	L	O	L	I	E	V	N	V	B	J	T	X	C	K	G
H	V	H	L	R	Y	L	E	-	F	V	P	R	K	W	T	R	I
O	C	L	C	S	T	R	N	X	X	R	D	Q	L	Y	S	E	L
L	W	N	C	O	S	N	I	X	Z	A	W	Y	W	I	X	U	Q
D	Q	T	V	I	O	S	X	P	M	A	J	O	J	W	Z	D	J
E	P	V	T	S	P	W	I	Z	N	F	I	R	Z	Q	J	N	N
R	F	Y	Y	A	R	T	H	S	A	E	L	B	A	T	R	O	P
F	L	Y	C	L	Z	F	K	Z	X	M	W	X	F	G	T	V	W

Find These Words

PATENTS
FLOWERS
SANITARYBELT
PORTABLEASHTRAY
TOILETPAPERHOLDER
BACKWASHER
HOWARDUNIVERSITY
SONN-NAP-PACK

Directions: Read and answer the questions. These are your opinions so the answers will vary.

Would you rather be famous for an invention or for something you've done?

What's your favorite color?

Share a special memory you have from school.

Directions: Read and answer the questions below. There are clues in the puzzle to help you. Try and solve the cryptic message.

Clue for cryptic message: Mary did this for a living.

Questions

1) Inventions ran in Mary's ____, her dad and grandfather both were inventers.

2) Mary has a patented the carrier attachment for a ____.

3) Mary was a federal ____ during World War II.

4) Mary holds the record (five) for the ____ number of patents awarded a Black woman by the U.S. government.

5) Mary invented an adjustable sanitary belt with a built-in ____-proof napkin pocket.

6) Mary held a patent on a back ____ that could be mounted on the shower or bathtub wall.

7) Mary patented a ____ paper holder that made sure the loose end of the roll was always reachable.

Directions: This is the WGLT Challenge. Solve the cryptogram. As the puzzle solver, you need to find which number belongs to which character. And this can be pretty challenging! You will need to match the number with the letter. There are some letters given to you below. This will help you solve the other words and unlock more characters. **Good Luck.**

Philip Downing

Philip Downing

**1857-1934
INVENTOR**

99

LEFT BLANK ON PURPOSE

Philip Downing

Philip Downing

Philip Downing

Philip Downing

Philip Downing

Philip Downing

Directions: read the bio below and answer the following questions.

Hi, my name is Philip Downing. I was born in 1857 in Providence, RI. I worked as a postal clerk for over 30 years in Boston, MA. During this time, if you wanted to send mail, you had to travel to the post office. I recognized that there was a need to help people who couldn't get to the post office on their own. In 1891, I got my second patent for a tall metal box with a secure, hinged door that could be used to post letters. This allowed drop-offs near individual homes and easy pick-up by a letter carrier. The hinged opening prevented rain or snow from entering the box and damaging the mail. A year before this, in 1890, I got my first patent for an electrical switch for railroads, which allowed railroad workers to supply or shut off power to trains at appropriate times. It also allowed the switches to be changed automatically in some cases. I received my third patent in 1917 for an envelope moistener, which utilized a roller and a small attached water tank to quickly moisten envelopes.

1. What did I do for work for over thirty years?
    A. Postal Master
    B. Postal Clerk
    C. Postal Driver
2. What year did I get my second patent?
    A. 1891
    B. 1890
    C. 1917
3. Which patent didn't have to do with the Post Office?
    A. Envelope moistener
    B. Mail box
    C. Electrical switch

Directions: Answer the questions, to solve the crossword puzzle. You can use the internet if you get stuck on any question.

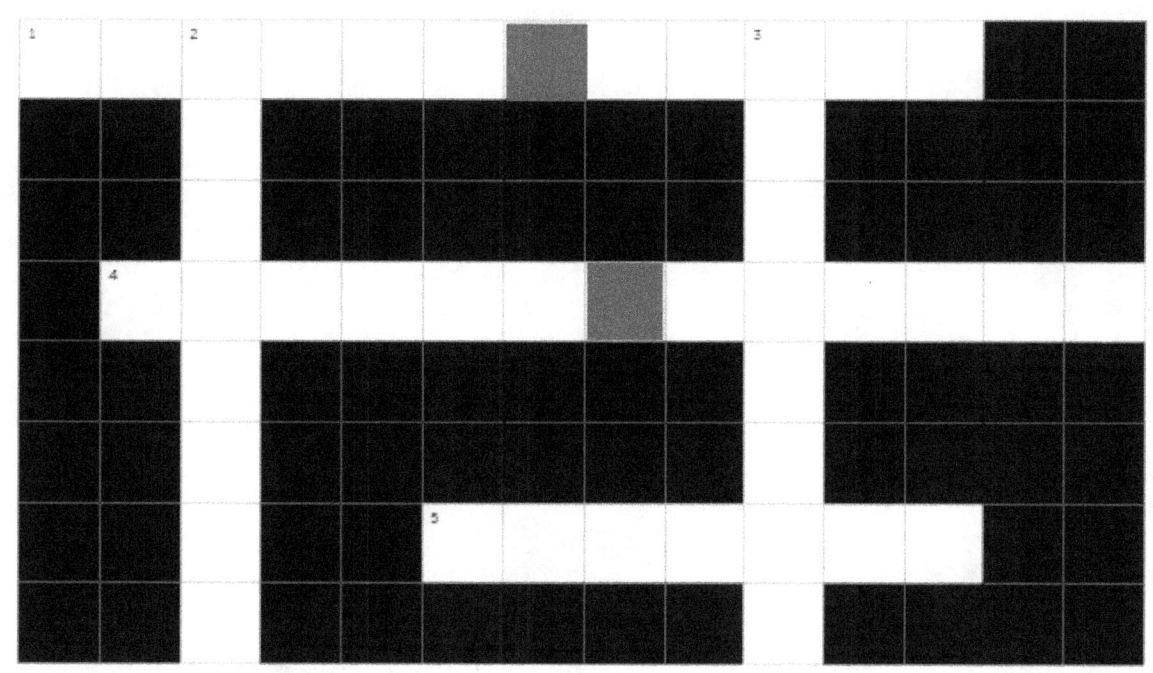

Across
1) Phillip retired from the post office after working for thirty-two years as a _____.
4) Phillip invented the _____ box, known as the mail box today.
5) Phillip invented a new type of desktop _____.

Down
2) Phillip invented a mechanical device for operating a street railway _____.
3) Phillip invented a handheld ___ moistener.

Directions: Read and answer the questions. These are your opinions so the answers will vary.

Would you rather play an individual or team sport?

What's your favorite genre of book to read?

What goals do you have for yourself? What are 5 things you want to do before you are (21)?

Directions: Unscramble the words below about Philip. See if you can get the bonus word.

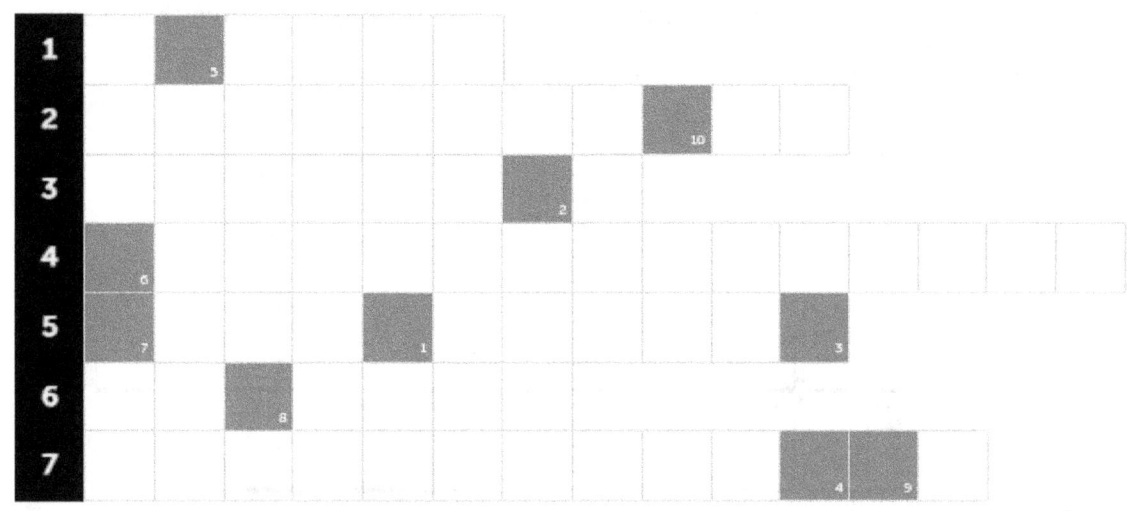

BONUS WORD

Unscramble Words

1) oostbn
2) tskocrlaelp
3) nitovner
4) grouotbfmlleaxe
5) tnspvitfeae
6) xbiolma
7) yrawtslihacwi

Directions: This is the WGLT Challenge. Solve the cryptogram. As the puzzle solver, you need to find which number belongs to which character. And this can be pretty challenging! You will need to match the number with the letter. There are some letters given to you below. This will help you solve the other words and unlock more characters. **Good Luck.**

Lewis Latimer

Lewis Latimer

September 4, 1848 – December 11, 1928
PATENT DRAFTSMAN

LEFT BLANK ON PURPOSE

Lewis Latimer

Lewis Latimer

Lewis Latimer

Lewis Latimer

Lewis Latimer

Lewis Latimer

Directions: read the bio below and answer the following questions.

Hi, my name is Lewis Latimer. I was born on September 4, 1848, in Chelsea, MA. I was 16 when I joined the U.S. Navy in 1864 during the Civil War. I served as a landsman on the USS Massasoit. In 1865, I received an honorable discharge. I got a job as an office boy with a patent law firm, Crosby, Halstead and Gould. I learned how to use a set square, ruler and other drafting tools. I used those skills for sketching patent drawings and became the firm's head draftsman in 1872. In 1874, I co-patented (with Charles M. Brown) an improved toilet system for railroad cars that was called the Water Closet for Railroad Cars. In 1881, I received a patent for the "Electric Lamp," which was an improved design for producing light using electricity and another in 1882 for the "Process of Manufacturing Carbons," which was an improved method for producing carbon filaments for lightbulbs. In 1884, I worked for The Edison Electric Light Company and in 1892, they merged with the Thomson-Houston Electric Company to form General Electric.

1. What war did I serve in?
    A. World War I
    B. Civil War
    C. World War II
2. Which invention of mine helped improve the light bulb?
    A. Water Closet for Railroad Cars
    B. Electric Lamp
    C. Process of Manufacturing Carbons
3. What ship did I serve on in the U.S. Navy?
    A. USS Massasoit
    B. USS Galena
    C. USS Monitor

Directions: Find the words associated with Lewis's life and career.

U	U	F	I	K	P	T	V	H	Y	H	T	D	R	H	F	Q	G
F	X	L	I	R	T	A	H	G	H	L	V	J	B	U	Y	W	V
S	R	D	E	Z	W	P	E	S	T	N	E	T	A	P	H	L	E
T	N	R	R	U	D	B	E	E	G	D	B	Y	Y	Y	W	W	S
N	Q	D	D	A	N	P	R	X	R	T	C	U	V	B	L	Q	D
E	B	V	B	V	F	Y	R	O	W	P	Y	W	M	A	H	O	T
M	E	D	M	M	V	T	T	O	H	S	B	K	E	P	N	C	T
A	J	Y	O	D	Z	N	S	R	K	T	I	T	X	Z	W	S	Z
L	H	B	I	V	E	X	R	M	U	I	U	P	C	D	H	C	U
I	B	J	S	V	M	I	P	L	A	X	T	A	J	L	B	U	C
F	H	J	N	C	D	D	S	C	V	N	L	Z	T	G	K	X	D
N	D	I	C	M	Y	D	A	R	X	G	L	F	M	F	S	K	K
O	T	A	I	R	C	O	N	D	I	T	I	O	N	E	R	R	R
B	V	W	W	C	P	X	D	R	E	E	N	I	G	N	E	C	C
R	D	S	W	T	O	I	L	E	T	S	Y	S	T	E	M	N	G
A	X	W	T	R	N	F	Q	I	W	Z	H	G	I	U	V	H	W
C	J	O	W	R	A	L	V	U	W	D	R	U	P	F	N	A	C
R	P	G	W	A	V	N	O	S	I	D	E	S	A	M	O	H	T

Find These Words

INVENTOR	USNAVY	DRAFTSMAN
CARBONFILAMENTS	TOILETSYSTEM	THOMASEDISON
AIRCONDITIONER	PATENTS	ENGINEER
AUTHOR		

Directions: Read and answer the questions. These are your opinions so the answers will vary.

Would you rather text your friends or get together?

What's your favorite story about your life so far?

Describe a situation where you showed extra kindness toward a stranger/friend.

Directions: Read and answer the questions below. There are clues in the puzzle to help you. Try and solve the cryptic message.

Clue for cryptic message: Lewis became one of these after the Navy.

Questions

1) Lewis helped Thomas _____ with his patent for the light bulb.
2) Lewis started working at _____ and Gould, a patent law firm.
3) Lewis severed in the U.S. _____ during the Civil War.
4) Lewis invented a better way to make carbon _____ for light bulbs.
5) Lewis was the first African American inventor and engineer to be given _____ patents for his innovative work.
6) Lewis's house is owned by the New York City Department of Parks & Recreation and is a member of the _____ House Trust.
7) Lewis invented an improved railroad car _____.
8) Lewis taught himself _____ drawing and drafting by observing the work of draftsmen at the firm and the firm partners promoted him from office boy to draftsman.
9) Lewis invented an early air _____ unit.

113

Directions: This is the WGLT Challenge. Solve the cryptogram. As the puzzle solver, you need to find which number belongs to which character. And this can be pretty challenging! You will need to match the number with the letter. There are some letters given to you below. This will help you solve the other words and unlock more characters. **Good Luck.**

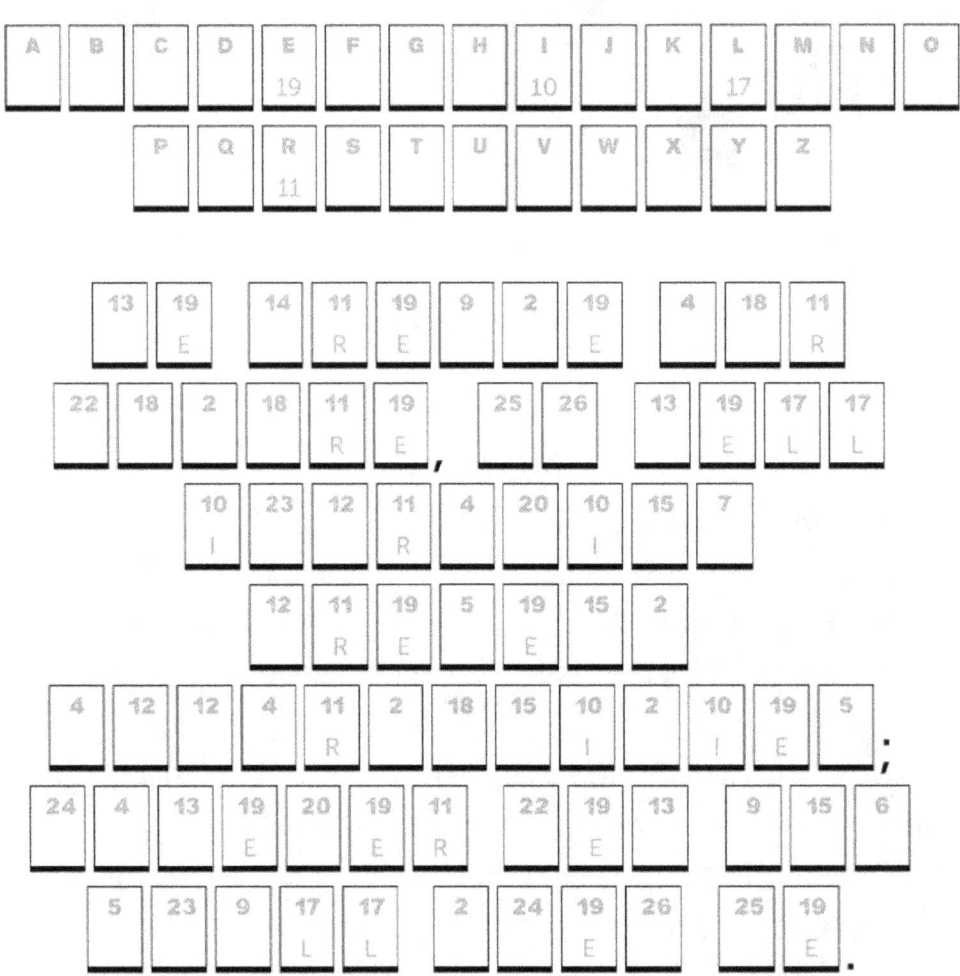

Henry T. Sampson

April 22, 1934 – June 4, 2015
ENGINEER

115

LEFT BLANK ON PURPOSE

Henry T. Sampson

Henry T. Sampson

Henry T. Sampson

Henry T. Sampson

Henry T. Sampson

Henry T. Sampson

Directions: read the bio below and answer the following questions.

Hi, my name is Henry T. Sampson Jr. I was born on April 22, 1934, in Jackson, MS. I graduated from Jackson's Lanier High School. I attended Morehouse College, but I transferred to Purdue University, which is where I got my bachelor's degree in chemical engineering. I became a member of the Omega Psi Phi fraternity. I earned my master's degree in engineering from the University of California. I got another master's degree and my Ph.D. in nuclear engineering from the University of Illinois Urbana-Champaign. I was the first African American to earn a Ph.D. in nuclear engineering in the United States. In 1964, I was awarded a patent for my Binder System for Propellants and Explosives. In 1971, I was awarded a patent with George H. Miley for the invention of the gamma-electric cell, which is a direct-conversion energy device that converts the energy generated from the radiation of high-energy gamma rays into electricity. In 1973, I invented an improved process for case-bonding propellant grains within a rocket chamber.

1. What fraternity am I a member of?
   A. Alpha Phi Alpha
   B. Omega Psi Phi
   C. Kappa Alpha Psi
2. What year did I get a patent for the gamma-electric cell?
   A. 1964
   B. 1973
   C. 1971
3. I was the first African American in the U.S. to what?
   A. Earn a PhD. in chemical engineering
   B. Earn a PhD. in music engineering
   C. Earn a PhD. in nuclear engineering

Directions: Answer the questions, to solve the crossword puzzle. You can use the internet if you get stuck on any question.

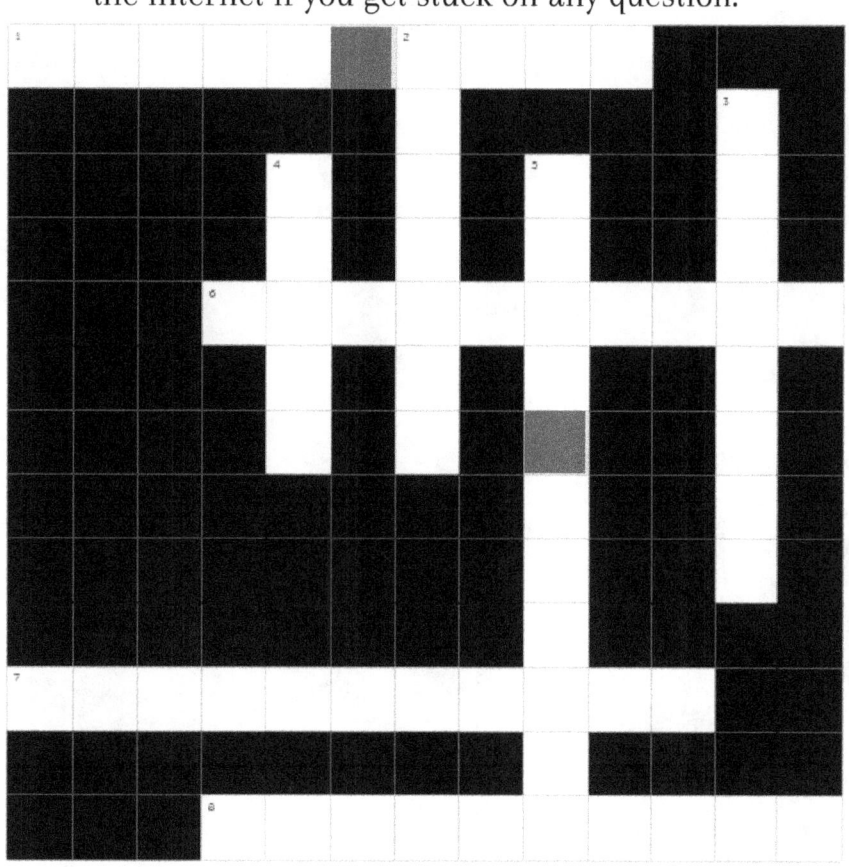

Across

1) Henry invented the gamma-electric cell which converted _____ into electricity.
6) Henry's research team focused on the powering and launching of _____.
7) Henry invented a binder system for _____.
8) Henry invented an ____ and a case bonding system for cast composite propellants.

Down

2) Henry invented materials that could help _____ propel.
3) Henry served as the _____ of Mission Development and Operations of the Space Test Program at the Aerospace Corporation.
4) Henry wrote a book entitled, "Blacks in ___ and White: A Source Book on Black Films."
5) Henry's invention inspired the creation of technology used in _____ and other devices for created power.

Directions: Read and answer the questions. These are your opinions so the answers will vary.

Would you rather be a wizard or a superhero?

What's your favorite video game?

Why do you think it is important to have rules in school?

Directions: Unscramble the words below about Henry. See if you can get the bonus word.

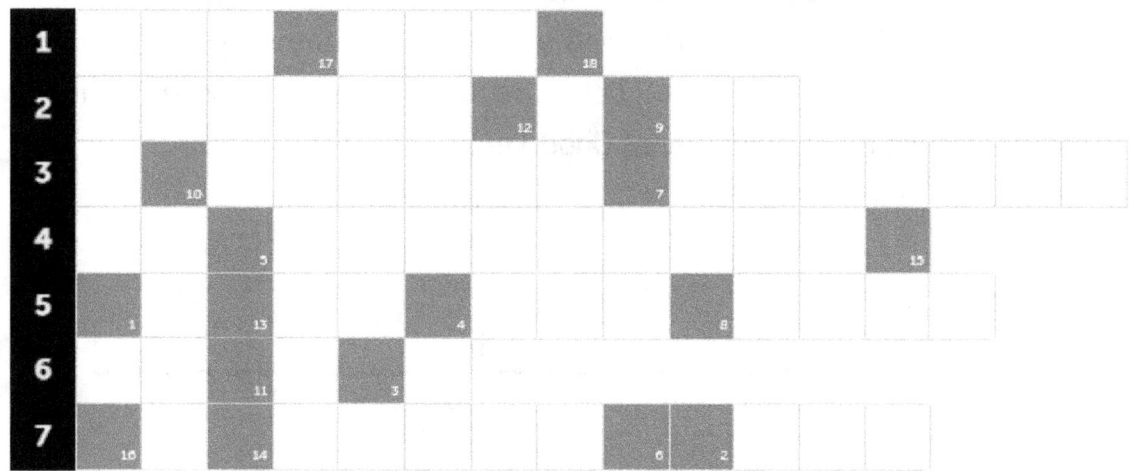

BONUS WORD

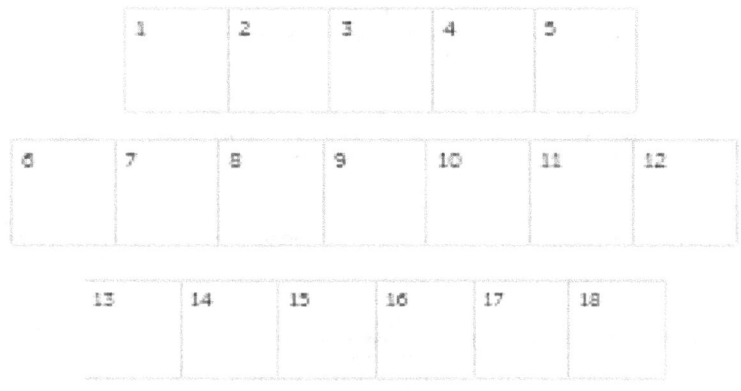

Unscramble Words

1) tiernnov
2) mhagoeiipps
3) egeourceoelslomh
4) tharifsnlmioi
5) acrlacenroetru
6) ynavsu
7) hgseaoshtkwtl

Directions: This is the WGLT Challenge. Solve the cryptogram. As the puzzle solver, you need to find which number belongs to which character. And this can be pretty challenging! You will need to match the number with the letter. There are some letters given to you below. This will help you solve the other words and unlock more characters. **Good Luck.**

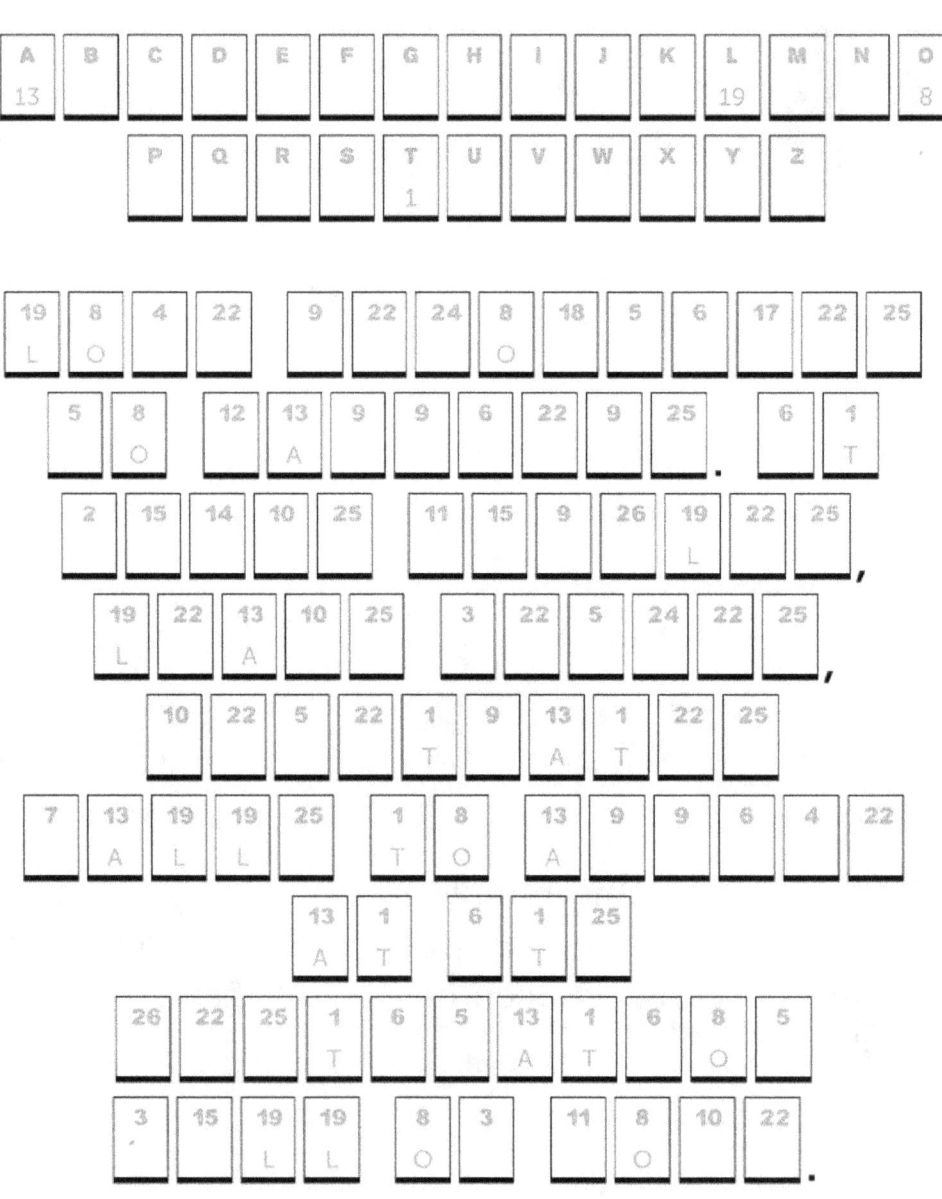

122

Madam C.J. Walker

Madam C.J. Walker

December 23, 1867 – May 25, 1919
ENTREPRENEUR

LEFT BLANK ON PURPOSE

Madam C.J. Walker

Madam C.J. Walker

Madam C.J. Walker

Madam C.J. Walker

Madam C.J. Walker

Madam C.J. Walker

Directions: read the bio below and answer the following questions.

Hi, my name is Sarah Breedlove. I was born on December 23, 1867, in Delta, LA. I got married at 14 and I had my one and only child, A'Lelia McWillams, in 1885. My family and I moved to St. Louis, MO, in 1888. I suffered from severe dandruff and baldness. I learned about hair care from my brothers, who were barbers. I became a commission agent who sold hair products for Annie Malone. In 1905, my daughter and I moved to Denver, CO, where I continued to sell products for Malone and develop my own hair-care business. In 1906, I married Charles Walker and became known as Madam C. J. Walker. I marketed myself as an independent hairdresser and retailer of cosmetic creams. I sold my products door to door and taught other Black women how to groom and style their hair. In 1910, I established a new base in Indianapolis. A'Lelia ran the day-to-day operations in Pittsburgh and we opened an office and beauty salon in the Harlem neighborhood in 1913; it became a center of African American culture.

1. Where did I learn about hair care?
   A. Annie Malone
   B. My Brothers
   C. My Parents
2. What year did I establish my base in Indianapolis?
   A. 1906
   B. 1908
   C. 1910
3. What made me want to learn about hair care?
   A. Severe dandruff
   B. My Daughters hair
   C. Baldness

Directions: Find the words associated with Madam C. J. Walker's life and career.

Z	Q	W	G	I	X	S	I	W	C	O	E	U	F	O	X	U	J
X	J	D	H	F	S	H	T	R	F	C	O	R	M	O	D	Z	B
A	I	V	Y	B	V	A	C	T	M	S	O	B	P	C	H	S	Z
N	Y	X	Y	G	S	M	X	M	M	X	V	T	Z	H	Z	L	H
R	K	F	A	G	P	P	W	J	A	M	A	I	C	A	P	O	G
A	K	Q	X	S	X	O	J	C	P	O	M	A	D	E	G	H	J
B	S	U	A	E	S	O	P	Y	A	W	D	W	G	M	E	W	I
F	S	X	H	D	I	Q	A	E	Q	X	W	P	Z	I	H	A	R
U	M	I	Q	W	L	L	N	J	L	Q	J	O	W	L	O	V	O
C	V	J	P	E	T	R	O	L	E	U	M	J	E	L	L	Y	N
S	O	C	I	A	L	A	C	T	I	V	I	S	T	I	V	T	C
J	E	D	C	N	T	V	F	B	V	B	E	R	E	O	Q	A	O
P	P	I	T	T	S	B	U	R	G	H	U	Z	W	N	N	K	M
Q	O	E	I	U	K	H	X	T	I	F	Y	J	Z	A	F	A	B
N	Y	K	P	W	K	B	Y	W	U	Z	X	Z	Z	I	L	H	A
M	Z	P	R	F	J	A	M	S	Q	L	F	J	V	R	L	K	M
A	D	Y	P	O	R	H	T	N	A	L	I	H	P	E	Z	A	E
U	L	E	W	H	F	K	V	F	R	J	U	M	B	W	W	K	J

Find These Words

SHAMPOO POMADE PETROLEUMJELLY
SUFUR PITTSBURGH JAMAICA
SOCIALACTIVIST IRONCOMB MILLIONAIRE
PHILANTHROPY

127

Directions: Read and answer the questions. These are your opinions so the answers will vary.

Would you rather play hide-and-seek or dodgeball?

Would you rather do your own hair or go to a barber or salon? Why?

What is one rule in all schools that you feel is unfair?

Directions: Read and answer the questions below. There are clues in the puzzle to help you. Try and solve the cryptic message.

Clue for cryptic message: Madam C. J. Walker was consider to be this.

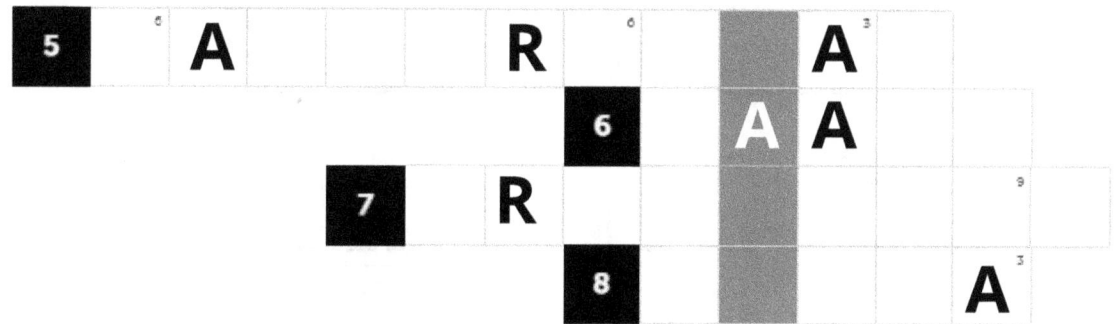

Questions

1) Madam C. J. Walker started working with hair care products because she began having problems with her own ____.

2) Madam C. J. Walker showed other black women how to ____, build their own businesses and encouraged them to become financially independent.

3) Madam C. J. Walker's famous shampoo contained ____ oil, lye and coconut oil.

4) Madam C. J. Walker was the first member of her family to be born ____.

5) Madam C. J. Walker use to work as a ____ while she lived in St. Louis, MO.

6) Madam C. J. Walker made financial donations to numerous organizations such as the ____ and YMCA.

7) Madam C. J. Walker's birth name was Sarah ____.

8) Madam C. J. Walker established ____ College to train "hair culturists" in Pittsburgh PA.

Directions: This is the WGLT Challenge. Solve the cryptogram. As the puzzle solver, you need to find which number belongs to which character. And this can be pretty challenging! You will need to match the number with the letter. There are some letters given to you below. This will help you solve the other words and unlock more characters. **Good Luck.**

A	B	C	D	E	F	G	H	I	J	K	L	M	N	O
22			26											14

P	Q	R	S	T	U	V	W	X	Y	Z
				17						

26 14 18 17 ' 21 20 17   26 14 8 18
D O _ T   _ _ T   D O _ _

22 18 26   8 22 20 17   3 14 19 17 11 12
A _ D   _ A _ T   _ O _ T _ _

14 6 6 14 19 17 10 18 20 17 20 12 21
O _ _ O _ T _ _ _ T _ _ _

17 14 13 14 23 12   25 12 17 10 6
T O _ O _ _   _ _ T _ _ .

22 18 26   23 22 2 12   17 11 12 23
A _ D   _ A _ _   T _ _ _

11 22 6 6 12 18
_ A _ _ _ _ .

130

Elijah McCoy

Elijah McCoy

May 2, 1844 – October 10, 1929
ENGINEER

LEFT BLANK ON PURPOSE

Elijah McCoy

Elijah McCoy

Elijah McCoy

Elijah McCoy

Elijah McCoy

Elijah McCoy

Directions: read the bio below and answer the following questions.

Hi, my name is Elijah J. McCoy. I was born on May 2, 1844, in Colchester, Ontario. I was certified as a mechanical engineer by the University of Edinburgh in Scotland. When I returned, my family had moved to Ypsilanti, MI. Due to racial barriers, I had to take a job as a fireman and oiler for the Michigan Central Railroad. Working there allowed me to see the inefficiencies that were inherent in the existing system for oiling axles. In 1872, I invented an automatic lubricator for oiling the steam engines of locomotives and ships. In 1898, I received another patent. I added a glass "sight-feed" tube to monitor the rate of lubricant delivery. By 1899, the Michigan Bureau of Labor and Industrial Statistics reported that the McCoy lubricator was in use on almost all North American railroads. The popular expression "the real McCoy," which typically means "the real thing," has been attributed to my oil-drip cup invention. One theory is that railroad engineers would request my invention by name and ask if a system was fitted with "the real McCoy system."

1. Where did I get certified as a mechanical engineer?
   A. University of Michigan
   B. Ontario Tech University
   C. University of Edinburgh
2. What year did I invent the automatic lubricator?
   A. 1872
   B. 1898
   C. 1899
3. What does the saying The real McCoy mean?
   A. Nickname
   B. Advertisement
   C. The real thing

Directions: Answer the questions, to solve the crossword puzzle. You can use the internet if you get stuck on any question.

Across

1) Elijah invented the _____ ironing board,
4) Elijah invented an automatic _____ for oiling the steam engines of ships.
5) Elijah was talked about in Booker T. Washington book Story of the _____ recognizing him as having produced more patents than any other black inventor up to that time.
7) Elijah invented and patented the first _____.
8) Elijah was inducted into the National _____ Hall of Fame.

Down

2) Elijah invented the _____ heels that prolonged the life of the shoe.
3) Elijah went to Edinburgh, ___ for an apprenticeship.
6) Elijah obtained more than fifty _____ in his life time.

135

Directions: Read and answer the questions. These are your opinions so the answers will vary.

Would you rather eat at home or in a restaurant?

_____

_____

What's your favorite activity to do with friends?

_____

_____

Do peers deserve the same respect as elders? Why?

_____

_____

_____

_____

_____

Directions: Unscramble the words below about Elijah. See if you can get the bonus word.

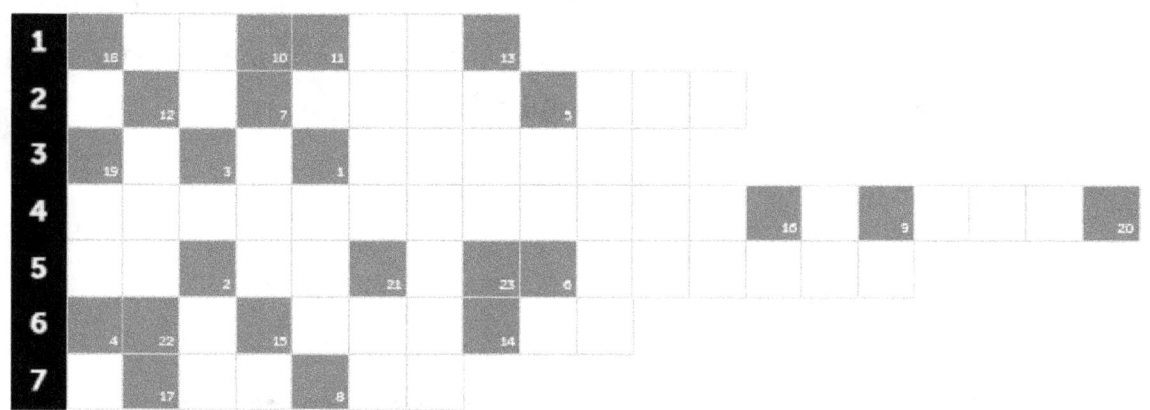

BONUS WORD

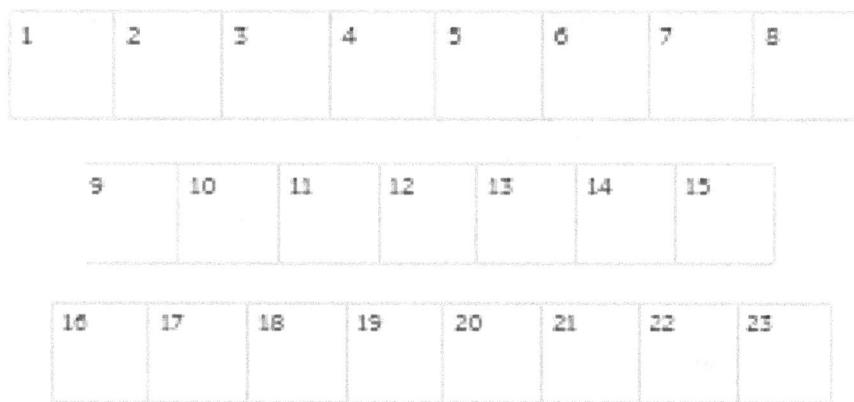

Unscramble Words

1) rnoinvet
2) mensitenegas
3) oitecoolvsm
4) tmbtotclaaouurcirai
5) zoegtailedatrar
6) hemllfoaaf
7) sptnaet

137

Directions: This is the WGLT Challenge. Solve the cryptogram. As the puzzle solver, you need to find which number belongs to which character. And this can be pretty challenging! You will need to match the number with the letter. There are some letters given to you below. This will help you solve the other words and unlock more characters. **Good Luck.**

Alexander Miles

Alexander Miles

May 18, 1838 – May 7, 1918
BUSINESSMAN

LEFT BLANK ON PURPOSE

Alexander Miles

Alexander Miles

Alexander Miles

Alexander Miles

Alexander Miles

Alexander Miles

Directions: read the bio below and answer the following questions.

Hi, my name is Alexander Miles. I was born on May 18, 1838, in Pickaway County, OH. For the most-part, I earned a living as a barber. I moved around a bit. I moved to Winona, MN and married Mrs. Candace J. (Shedd) Dunlap. In 1876, our daughter Grace was born and we moved to Duluth, MN, where I became the first Black member of the Duluth Chamber of Commerce. I operated a barber shop out of the St. Louis Hotel. After Grace accidentally fell down an elevator shaft, which almost ended her life, I came up with an invention for automatically opening and closing elevator doors in 1887. This was a more efficient way to operate elevators. Before this, the doors of both the shaft and the elevator had to be opened and closed manually by either the elevator operator or by passengers, which contributed greatly to the hazards of operating an elevator. In 1899, I founded The United Brotherhood as a life insurance company that insured Black people, who were often denied coverage at that time.

1. What did I do to make a living?
    A. Invent things
    B. Work in the Chamber of Commerce
    C. Barber
2. What year did I patent automatic elevator doors?
    A. 1881
    B. 1890
    C. 1887
3. What made me want to invent automatic elevator doors?
    A. Tired of closing them manually
    B. Make them easy to operate
    C. My daughter falling down the shaft

Directions: Find the words associated with Alexander's life and career.

H	A	L	L	O	F	F	A	M	E	U	V	M	K	D	A	B	U
C	H	H	X	P	T	X	I	G	H	Q	U	L	U	A	T	V	P
C	A	R	M	M	L	G	N	S	R	N	U	N	B	O	A	G	C
Q	I	O	F	Q	I	C	S	X	M	A	Y	B	U	F	M	S	S
B	R	B	S	E	S	T	U	Q	E	V	L	Y	K	E	R	R	B
U	C	Q	J	A	F	C	R	R	A	L	Z	W	Q	W	P	O	H
S	A	P	K	V	P	I	A	S	C	L	C	P	E	G	O	O	J
I	R	I	C	Q	A	I	N	Z	J	Q	Q	Z	T	T	M	D	H
N	E	J	S	D	T	Y	C	V	G	P	S	S	X	U	L	R	V
E	P	R	E	R	E	C	E	V	E	N	S	S	F	G	Q	O	J
S	R	E	A	J	N	E	C	Y	G	N	W	B	X	C	D	T	Z
S	O	B	T	R	T	P	O	N	I	A	T	I	C	K	A	A	P
M	D	R	T	U	S	M	M	H	W	X	H	O	W	O	X	V	Z
A	U	A	L	Z	W	H	P	N	P	F	G	X	R	K	N	E	P
N	C	B	E	Z	O	V	A	B	M	F	F	S	U	Y	J	L	P
T	T	A	J	W	A	S	N	B	G	W	K	T	H	K	Q	E	X
P	K	N	R	Z	Y	K	Y	T	D	N	R	P	A	Y	P	N	X
X	U	N	T	I	G	C	E	C	H	I	C	A	G	O	M	J	O

Find These Words

INVENTOR   CHICAGO   BARBER
PATENTS   HALLOFFAME   INSURANCECOMPANY
ELEVATORDOORS BUSINESSMAN   SEATTLE
HAIRCAREPRODUCT

Directions: Read and answer the questions. These are your opinions so the answers will vary.

Would you rather visit the mountains or the ocean?

What's your favorite show on TV?

How do you prefer others show kindness- hugs, notes, time together, etc?

144

Directions: Read and answer the questions below. There are clues in the puzzle to help you. Try and solve the cryptic message.

Clue for cryptic message: Alexander did this for a living.

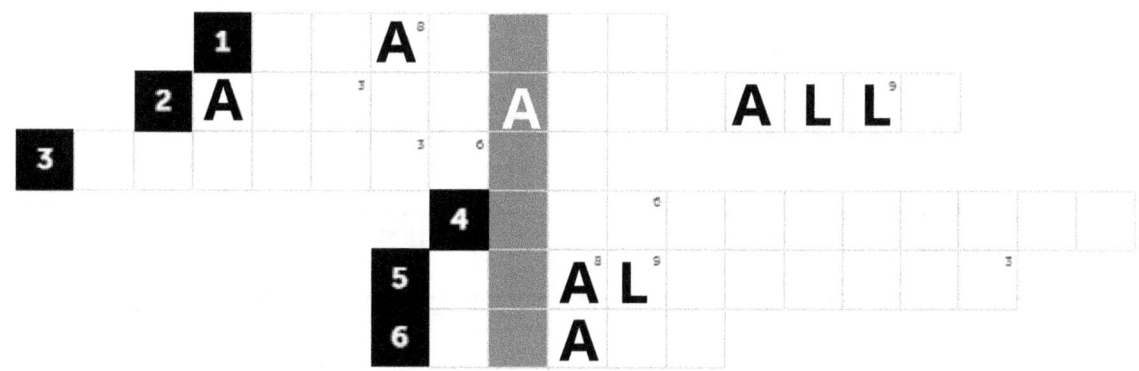

Questions

1) Alexander the first African-American member of the Duluth _____ of Commerce.
2) Alexander patented his design for improving the _____ opening and closing elevator doors.
3) Alexander was inducted into the National _____ Hall of Fame.
4) Alexander founded The United _____, a life insurance company.
5) Alexander was the _____ African American in the Pacific Northwest region.
6) Alexander got the idea for the automatic elevator doors when his daughter _____ accidentally fell down a shaft, almost ending her life.

Directions: This is the WGLT Challenge. Solve the cryptogram. As the puzzle solver, you need to find which number belongs to which character. And this can be pretty challenging! You will need to match the number with the letter. There are some letters given to you below. This will help you solve the other words and unlock more characters. **Good Luck.**

Charles Drew

Charles Drew

June 3, 1904 – April 1, 1950
SURGEON

LEFT BLANK ON PURPOSE

Charles Drew

Charles Drew

Charles Drew

Charles Drew

Charles Drew

Charles Drew

Directions: read the bio below and answer the following questions.

Hi, my name is Charles Drew. I was born on June 3, 1904, in Washington, D.C. I graduated from Washington's Dunbar High School. I graduated from Amherst College. In 1926, I became a professor of chemistry and biology at the historically Black Morgan College. In 1933, I graduated with a Doctorate of Medicine and Master of Surgery degree from McGill University's Faculty of Medicine. I also became a member of Alpha Omega Alpha. I earned a Doctorate of Science and Surgery from Columbia University. I was the first African American to get a doctorate from Columbia. In 1941, I worked on developing a blood bank that was to be used for U.S. military personnel. But I became frustrated with the military's request for segregating the blood that was donated by African Americans. At first, the military did not want to use blood from African Americans, but they later said it could only be used for African American soldiers. I resigned because of this racist policy. In 1942, I received a patent for preserving blood.

1. What college did I get my doctorate from?
    A. Amherst College
    B. Morgan College
    C. Columbia University
2. What year did I get patent for Preserving Blood?
    A. 1941
    B. 1942
    C. 1945
3. What HBCU was I a professor at?
    A. Fisk University
    B. Morgan College
    C. Morehouse College

Directions: Answer the questions, to solve the crossword puzzle. You can use the internet if you get stuck on any question.

Across

1) Charles developed improved ____ for blood storage.

5) Charles the first African-American ____ selected to serve as an examiner on the American Board of Surgery.

6) Charles achieved membership in Alpha ____ Alpha, a scholastic honor society for medical students.

7) Charles was the first ____ at Morgan College.

8) Charles started what would be later known as ____.

Down

2) Charles was appointed medical ____ of the "Plasma for Britain" project.

3) Charles was the director of the newly formed ____ Blood Bank.

4) Charles played on the ____ as well as the track and field team for Amherst College.

Directions: Read and answer the questions. These are your opinions so the answers will vary.

Would you rather have art or PE?

What's your favorite activity to do with family?

Why do you think it is important to have rules in society?

Directions: Unscramble the words below about Charles. See if you can get the bonus word.

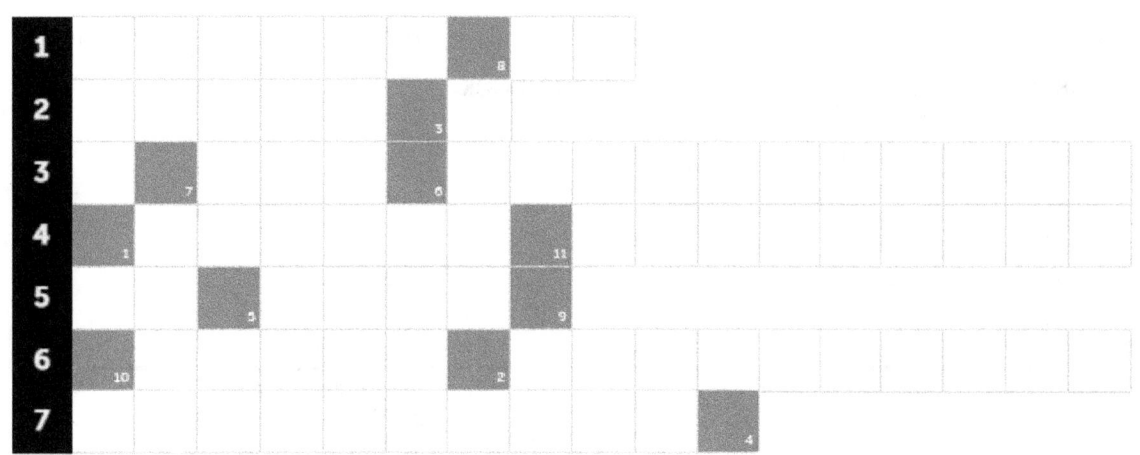

BONUS WORD

Unscramble Words
1) bdaknolbo
2) oesgrun
3) eiovrtodolbsreanp
4) sfrssanoliutnodbo
5) osrrdecs
6) eeieamlrahdrerscc
7) oldwtrorwwa

153

Directions: This is the WGLT Challenge. Solve the cryptogram. As the puzzle solver, you need to find which number belongs to which character. And this can be pretty challenging! You will need to match the number with the letter. There are some letters given to you below. This will help you solve the other words and unlock more characters. **Good Luck.**

November 4, 1942 – May 30, 2019
OPHTHALMOLOGIST

LEFT BLANK ON PURPOSE

Patricia Bath

Patricia Bath

Patricia Bath

Patricia Bath

Patricia Bath

Patricia Bath

Directions: read the bio below and answer the following questions.

Hi, my name is Patricia Bath. I was born on November 4, 1942, in Harlem, NY. I graduated from Charles Evans Hughes High School. I got a Bachelor of Science in Chemistry from Hunter College. I graduated with honors from Howard University College of Medicine. I began my career by becoming the first woman ophthalmologist on the faculty at Jules Stein Eye Institute at UCLA. In 1978, I founded the Ophthalmic Assistant Training Program (OATP). The graduates of the OATP are key personnel who provide screening, health education, and support for blindness prevention strategies. In 1983, I was appointed the chair of the KING-DREW-UCLA Ophthalmology Residency Program, which made me the first woman in the US to head an ophthalmology residency program. In 1986, I invented the Laserphaco Probe, which improved treatment for cataract patients. I patented the device in 1988 and became the first African American female doctor to receive a medical patent.

1. What college did I get my Bachelors degree from?
    A. Hunter College
    B. Howard University
    C. Columbia University
2. What year did I patent Laserphaco Probe?
    A. 1986
    B. 1988
    C. 1983
3. I was the first African American female in the U.S. to?
    A. Get my Ph.D in medicine
    B. Graduate from Howard University College of Medicine
    C. Receive a medical patent

Directions: Find the words associated with Patricia's life and career.

H	U	M	A	N	I	T	A	R	I	A	N	C	G	E	V	V	N
X	C	O	P	H	T	H	A	L	M	O	L	O	G	Y	D	M	I
G	G	T	R	E	C	N	A	C	-	T	C	I	D	E	R	P	U
W	A	I	A	Q	M	M	E	W	B	G	R	N	X	Y	O	N	C
S	R	H	Q	N	X	T	C	V	I	C	R	K	J	T	J	K	D
T	U	B	A	U	Z	K	C	G	T	N	M	P	Y	V	V	L	O
N	E	U	C	N	F	A	H	N	T	T	V	D	G	B	O	B	H
E	B	D	V	F	Z	U	N	P	S	O	K	E	J	R	V	F	U
T	G	H	I	O	T	U	L	I	S	S	U	Y	N	R	I	O	Q
A	F	P	V	O	F	A	Z	A	A	V	R	F	D	T	Z	Q	O
P	C	E	K	A	E	M	J	Q	S	N	C	Z	C	X	O	V	P
W	Y	Z	W	Z	P	Y	C	F	N	E	C	R	Q	B	J	R	B
U	Z	R	N	E	K	C	P	K	L	W	R	G	G	N	O	J	G
Q	N	U	A	E	R	U	B	-	S	N	E	R	D	L	I	H	C
J	T	X	A	Z	I	K	R	G	X	P	W	J	B	G	A	O	T
Y	X	U	L	W	I	K	L	D	D	C	U	M	C	U	L	N	V
U	B	F	P	Q	C	A	T	A	R	A	C	T	S	P	U	Q	X
A	B	L	I	N	D	N	E	S	S	N	W	D	S	R	P	Z	Y

Find These Words

CATARACTS   LASER   TANZANIA
OPHTHALMOLOGY   INVENTOR   HUMANITARIAN
PATENTS   BLINDNESS   PREDICT-CANCER
CHILDRENS-BUREAU

Directions: Read and answer the questions. These are your opinions so the answers will vary.

If you could travel anywhere in our solar system, where would you go?

What's your favorite meal of the day?

Have you volunteered in your community?

Directions: Read and answer the questions below. There are clues in the puzzle to help you. Try and solve the cryptic message.

Clue for cryptic message: Patricia went here at some point.

Questions

1) Patricia was the first African-American person to serve as a resident in _____ at New York University.
2) Patricia co-founded in 1976 with Alfred Cannon and Aaron Ifekwunigwe the American Institute for the _____ of Blindness.
3) Patricia the first ___ member of the Jules Stein Eye Institute.
4) Patricia patented a method for using pulsed _____ to remove cataracts.
5) Patricia first woman to lead a _____ training program in ophthalmology.
6) Patricia was the first African-American woman ___ to receive a patent for a medical purpose holding five patents altogether.

Directions: This is the WGLT Challenge. Solve the cryptogram. As the puzzle solver, you need to find which number belongs to which character. And this can be pretty challenging! You will need to match the number with the letter. There are some letters given to you below. This will help you solve the other words and unlock more characters. **Good Luck.**

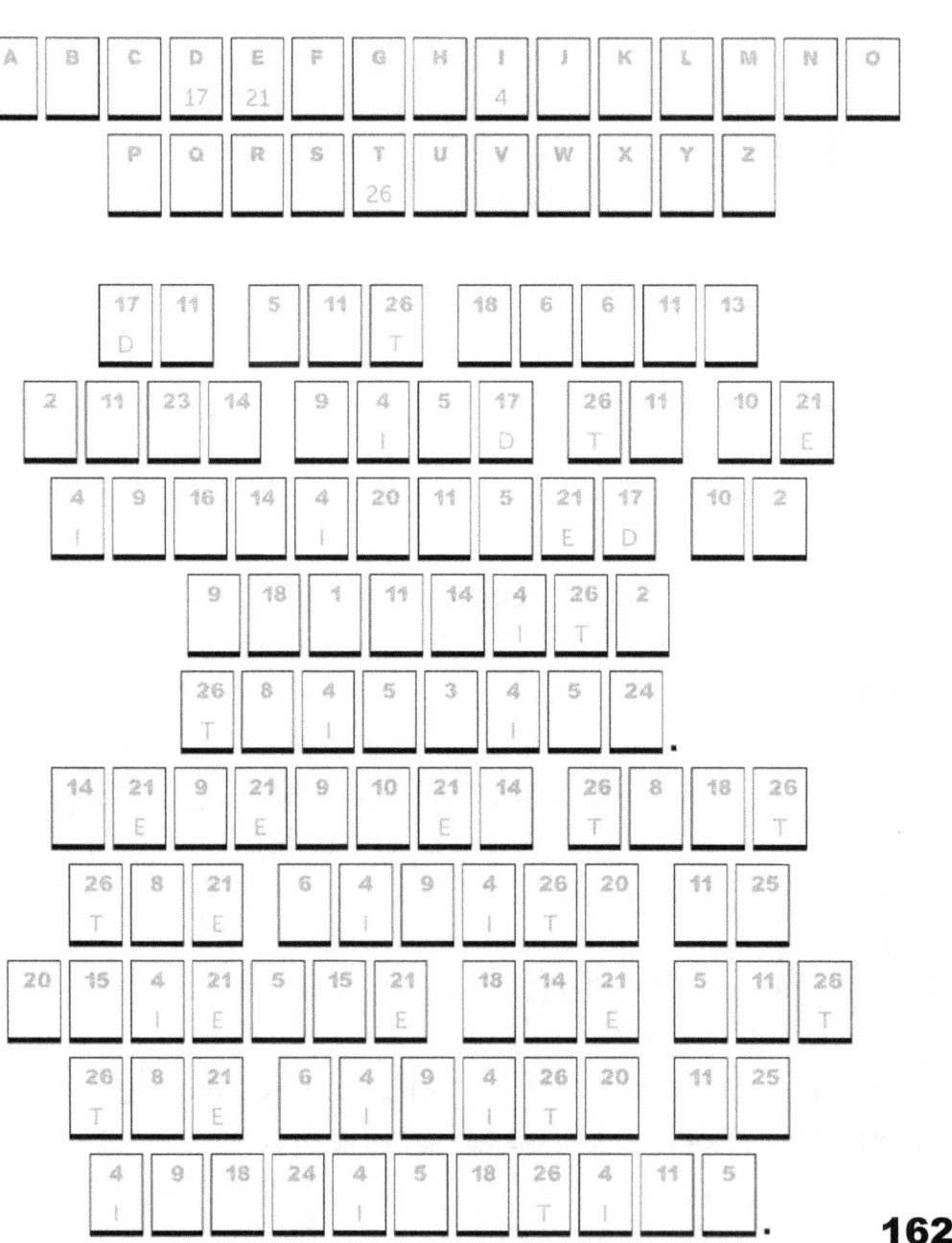

Wallace Amos

Wallace Amos

July 1, 1936 –PRESENT
TV PERSONALITY

LEFT BLANK ON PURPOSE

Wallace Amos

Wallace Amos

Wallace Amos

Wallace Amos

Wallace Amos

Wallace Amos

Directions: read the bio below and answer the following questions.

Hi, my name is Wallace Amos Jr. I was born on July 1, 1936, in Tallahassee, FL. I dropped out of high school to join the United States Air Force. I earned my GED while serving in the military. In 1957, I joined the William Morris Agency, where I worked my way up from the mailroom to become the first Black talent agent in the industry. I signed Simon and Garfunkel and worked with Motown megastars The Supremes, Sam Cooke and Marvin Gaye. I went to meetings with record-company or movie people and always brought along some cookies. Pretty soon, everybody was asking for them. My brand got backing from celebrity investors such as Marvin Gaye and Helen Reddy, who gave me $25,000 for my new business. In 1975, I opened the first Famous Amos cookie store in Los Angeles, CA. The company began to expand and eventually, Famous Amos chocolate chip cookies could be found on supermarket shelves across the United States. I'm the creator of the Famous Amos chocolate chip cookie.

1. What branch of the service was I in?
    A. Air Force
    B. Marine Corps
    C. Army
2. What year did I open my first store?
    A. 1980
    B. 1975
    C. 1970
3. I'm the founder of what cookie?
    A. Keebler Fudge Stripes
    B. Famous Amos chocolate-chip cookie
    C. Chips Ahoy chocolate-chip cookie

Directions: Answer the questions, to solve the crossword puzzle. You can use the internet if you get stuck on any question.

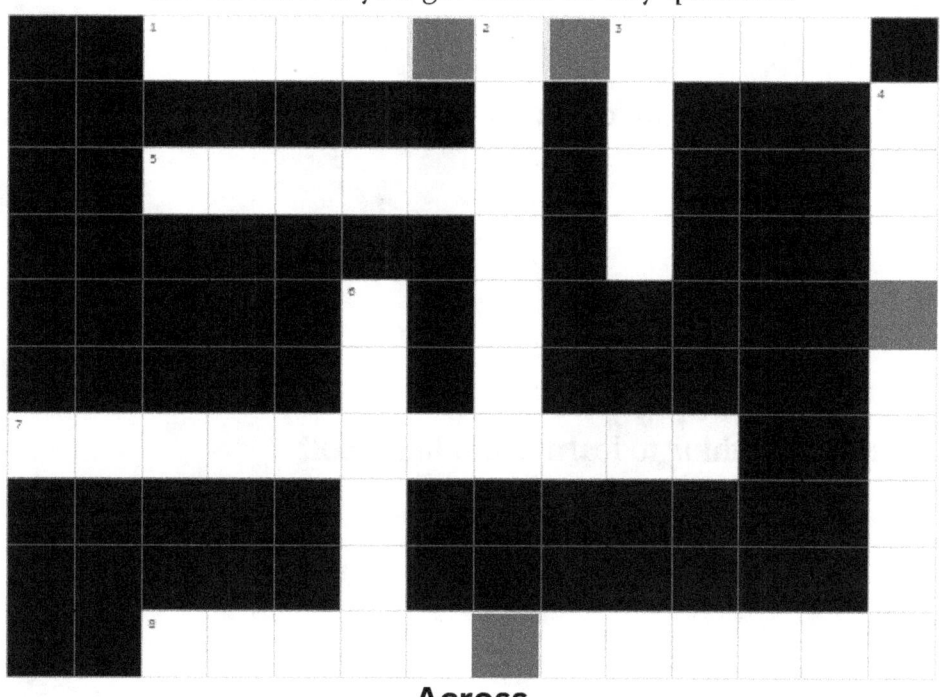

Across

1) Wally worked for William Morris Agency and headed the agency's ____ department.

5) Wally's Uncle Noname became Uncle Wally's ____ Company focused on fat-free, nutritious muffins.

7) Wally appeared in the tv sitcom The Office as himself, in the episode _____.

8) Wally has a documentary called The _____ Comeback: reBaking Wally Amos.

Down

2) Wally had to use The Uncle _____ Cookie Company as his new company's name.

3) Wally hosted a television series designed to teach others how to read, entitled Learn to ____.

4) Wally join the United States _____ and served at Hickam Air Force Base in Honolulu, HI.

6) Wally bought back his handmade cookies under a new name The Cookie ____ in 2014.

Directions: Read and answer the questions. These are your opinions so the answers will vary.

If you could meet a musician or group, who would it be?

What's your favorite thing to learn about in school?

In your free time, what do you like to do?

Directions: Unscramble the words below about Wallace. See if you can get the bonus word.

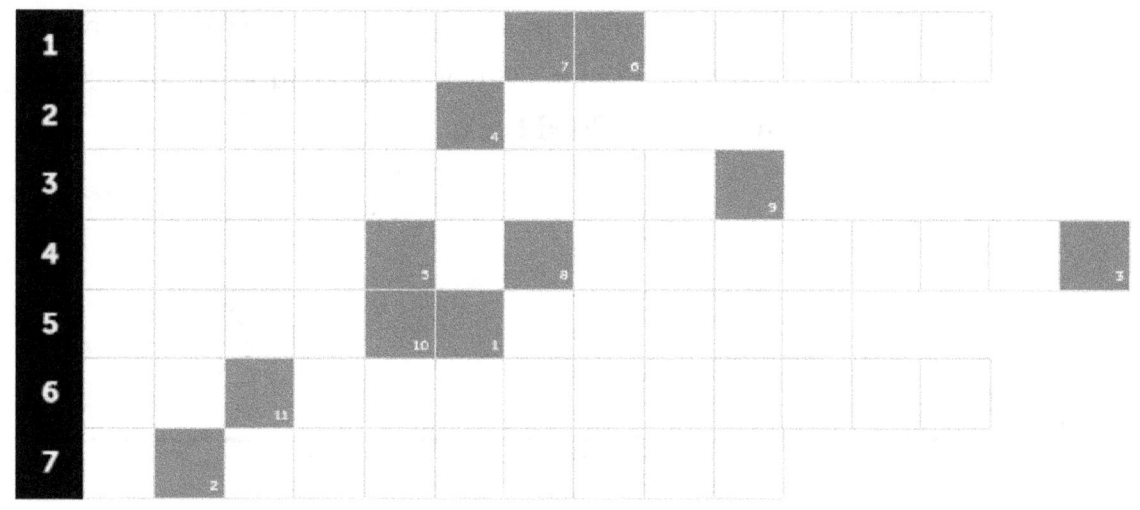

BONUS WORD

Unscramble Words

1) ihcaptechlooc
2) skecoio
3) rrsocfueia
4) usgfaeorilk&nmn
5) eaneoltrdra
6) oesskiaaocLkt
7) saoaumsfmo

Directions: This is the WGLT Challenge. Solve the cryptogram. As the puzzle solver, you need to find which number belongs to which character. And this can be pretty challenging! You will need to match the number with the letter. There are some letters given to you below. This will help you solve the other words and unlock more characters. **Good Luck.**

170

Majorie S. Joyner

October 24, 1896 – December 27, 1994
HAIR CARE ENTREPRENEUR

171

LEFT BLANK ON PURPOSE

Majorie S. Joyner

Majorie S. Joyner

Majorie S. Joyner

Majorie S. Joyner

Majorie S. Joyner

Majorie S. Joyner

Directions: read the bio below and answer the following questions.

Hi, my name is Marjorie Stewart. I was born on October 24, 1896, in Monterey, VA. I studied cosmetology and graduated from A.B. Molar Beauty School in 1916. I was the first African American to graduate from the school. I received my bachelor's degree in psychology from Bethune-Cookman College. I worked for Madam C. J. Walker as a sales representative. In 1920, I oversaw 200 of Madam Walker's beauty schools as the national adviser. I taught some 15,000 stylists and worked as an instructor by coaching Walker's door-to-door sales representatives. In 1928, I invented and patented the permanent wave machine that could be used to set a hairdo for days. The patent was credited to Walker's company and I received almost no money for it. In 1945, I, along with Mary McLeod Bethune, founded the United Beauty School Owners and Teachers Association, which is a national association for African American beauticians.

1. **Which HBCU did I graduate from?**
   A. **Spelman College**
   B. **Fisk University**
   C. **Bethune-Cookman College**
2. **What did I invent in 1928?**
   A. **Curling Iron**
   B. **Permanent wave machine**
   C. **Hot comb**
3. **What did myself and Mary McLeod Bethune found?**
   A. **NAACP**
   B. **United Barbers Assoc**
   C. **United Beauty School Owners and Teachers Assoc**

Directions: Find the words associated with Marjorie's life and career.

Z	H	R	E	D	N	E	F	E	D	O	G	A	C	I	H	C	K
A	F	R	W	M	W	W	K	D	T	I	J	X	H	M	L	V	Q
A	G	B	G	W	A	V	E	M	A	C	H	I	N	E	U	T	X
P	D	A	U	P	R	F	I	Q	H	C	F	F	E	Y	E	N	H
H	L	H	O	S	S	L	L	Q	H	V	P	Q	Q	K	P	A	L
I	I	Y	A	Z	I	Y	A	U	Y	M	Y	Q	J	I	W	M	A
L	R	R	B	I	W	N	C	D	F	Z	D	I	S	K	J	K	Q
A	O	Z	H	A	R	K	E	H	N	O	L	A	S	B	S	O	Z
N	T	X	C	C	M	C	W	S	O	G	T	R	V	P	H	O	J
T	A	E	F	G	O	C	A	R	S	L	F	R	Q	X	G	C	L
H	C	Q	W	Y	J	J	W	R	Z	W	O	S	L	F	Z	-	H
R	U	J	R	V	B	E	P	A	E	R	O	G	S	O	G	E	B
O	D	N	L	B	O	P	M	Y	K	X	S	M	Y	V	R	N	R
P	E	J	I	K	D	D	X	R	P	U	Q	V	A	X	D	U	M
I	U	T	S	I	V	I	T	C	A	R	R	J	Y	N	R	H	P
S	B	T	Q	H	R	M	U	V	A	E	G	M	Z	W	M	T	C
T	X	R	J	T	Q	F	H	D	X	S	O	C	L	W	D	E	K
V	H	T	S	O	G	V	O	T	M	W	Q	L	X	K	K	B	G

Find These Words

CHICAGODEFENDER   SALON   BUSINESSWOMAN
PSYCHOLOGY   BETHUNE-COOKMAN   PHILANTHROPIST
WAVEMACHINE   EDUCATOR   ACTIVIST
HAIRCARE

175

Directions: Read and answer the questions. These are your opinions so the answers will vary.

If you could meet a historical figure, who would it be?

What's your favorite extracurricular class?

What is your favorite thing to do over the weekends?

Directions: Read and answer the questions below. There are clues in the puzzle to help you. Try and solve the cryptic message.

Clue for cryptic message: Marjorie went here later in life.

Questions

1) Marjorie patented a ___ protector to make the procedure more comfortable.
2) Marjorie got her inspiration from a ____ cooking with paper pins to quicken preparation time.
3) Marjorie's invention was readily adopted by ____, which were able to help both black and white clients to straighten or curl their hair.
4) Marjorie has an exhibit at the Smithsonian Institution featuring her permanent wave machine and a ____ of her original salon.
5) Marjorie helped found a sorority and fraternity dedicated to the advancement and promotion of the ____ industry, Alpha Chi Pi Omega.
6) Marjorie opened a salon on South State Street in ____ after graduating from A.B. Molar Beauty School.
7) Marjorie serving as head of the Chicago ____ Charity network

Directions: This is the WGLT Challenge. Solve the cryptogram. As the puzzle solver, you need to find which number belongs to which character. And this can be pretty challenging! You will need to match the number with the letter. There are some letters given to you below. This will help you solve the other words and unlock more characters. **Good Luck.**

178

December 1, 1940 – April 9, 2011
ELECTRONIC ENGINEER

179

LEFT BLANK ON PURPOSE

Gerald Lawson

Gerald Lawson

Gerald Lawson

Gerald Lawson

Gerald Lawson

Gerald Lawson

Directions: read the bio below and answer the following questions.

Hi, my name is Gerald Lawson. I was born on December 1, 1940, in Brooklyn, NY. When I was 13, I gained an amateur ham radio license and then built my own station at home with parts from local electronic stores. I attended both Queens College and City College of New York but did not graduate from either one. In 1970, I joined Fairchild Semiconductor as an application engineering consultant within their sales division. In 1975, I created an early version of the coin-operated arcade game, which I called Demolition Derby, in my garage by using Fairchild's new F8 microprocessors. Demolition Derby was among the earliest microprocessor-driven games. I led the development of the Fairchild Channel F console, which was released in 1976 and was specifically designed to use swappable game cartridges based on technology that was licensed from Alpex. At the time, most game systems had game programming built into the hardware, so it could not be removed or changed. They call me the "Father of the Videogame Cartridge."

1. What college didn't I go to?
    A. Queens College
    B. New York University
    C. City College of New York
2. What is the name of the arcade game I created?
    A. Pac Man
    B. Frogger
    C. Demolition Derby
3. What is my nickname?
    A. Father of microprocessors
    B. Father of the videogame cartridge
    C. Father of the coin arcade

Directions: Answer the questions, to solve the crossword puzzle. You can use the internet if you get stuck on any question.

Across

1) Jerry was a member of the Homebrew _____, a group of early computer hobbyists that included several who became well-known including Apple founders Steve Jobs and Steve Wozniak.

3) Jerry led the development of the Fairchild _____ with a new 8-way joystick and a "pause" button, which was a first for a home video game console.

4) Jerry was honored as an industry ___ for his work on the game cartridge concept by the International Game Developers Association.

5) Jerry first-grade teacher encouraged him on his path to be someone _____, similar to George Washington Carver.

6) Jerry interests in scientific hobbies, including ham radio and _____.

7) Jerry _____ games for Atari in the 80's and felt they should be used as teaching tools.

Down

1) Jerry created an early _____ arcade game called Demolition Derby in his garage in 1975.

2) Jerry was an applications _____ consultant within Fairchild Semiconductor sales division.

Directions: Read and answer the questions. These are your opinions so the answers will vary.

If you could go back to any period in time, which would you choose?

What's your favorite breakfast food?

What is a unique talent you have?

Directions: Unscramble the words below about Gerald. See if you can get the bonus word.

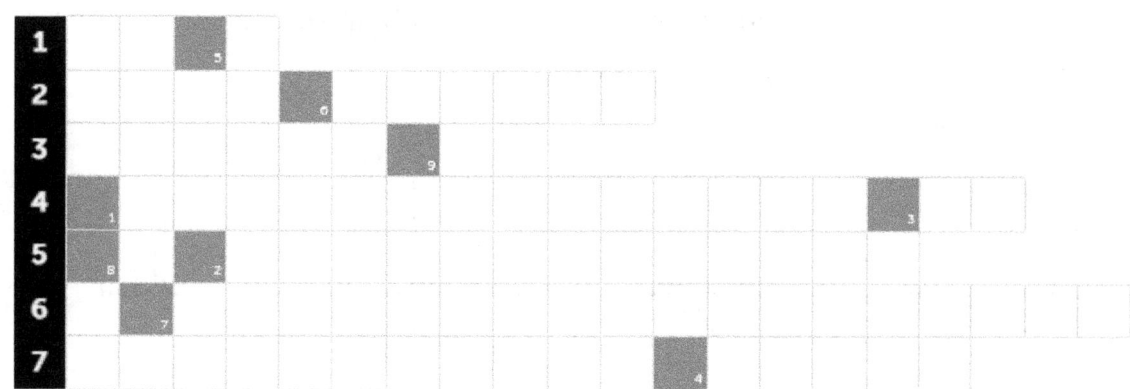

BONUS WORD

1	2	3	4	5	6	7	8	9

Unscramble Words

1) xxob
2) lytasiapton
3) scyhmietr
4) revtgargdaiieomedc
5) adcinhfciehrnalf
6) uoeblmorhberetmcwucp
7) is8pocoefrrsromcs

185

Directions: This is the WGLT Challenge. Solve the cryptogram. As the puzzle solver, you need to find which number belongs to which character. And this can be pretty challenging! You will need to match the number with the letter. There are some letters given to you below. This will help you solve the other words and unlock more characters. **Good Luck.**

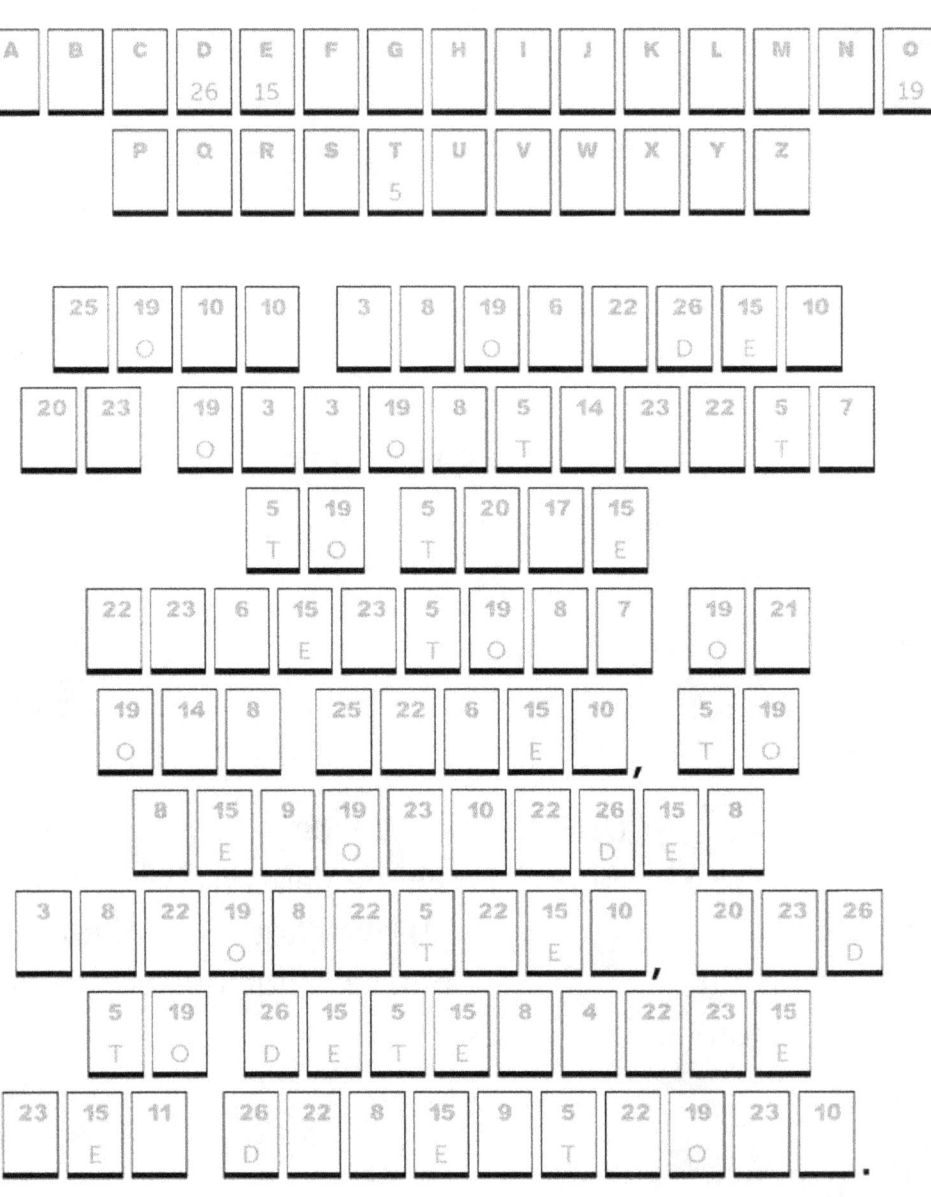

186

Sarah Boone

Sarah Boone

1832 – 1904
INVENTOR

Sarah Boone

Sarah Boone

Sarah Boone

Sarah Boone

Sarah Boone

Sarah Boone

Directions: read the bio below and answer the following questions.

Hi, my name is Sarah Marshall. I was born in 1832 in Craven County, NC. I was born into slavery and prevented from having a formal education. Instead, I was educated by my grandfather at home. In 1847, I married James Boone, who was a free Black man, in New Bern and I was granted freedom from slavery. My husband and I moved to New Haven, CT, before the outbreak of the American Civil War. I worked as a dressmaker. It was illegal to teach African Americans to read and write at that time, but I finally took steps to overcome that disadvantage in my late 40s through my church. There was fierce competition in my field. I had to find a way for my dresses to catch the eyes of customers. I created a narrower, curved board that could be slipped into sleeves and used to shift a garment without wrinkling it. It was also padded to eliminate the impressions that would be produced by a wooden board and collapsible for easy storage. In 1892, I obtained a patent for my improvements to the ironing board.

1. Who did I receive my education from?
   A. High School Teacher
   B. Grandmother
   C. Grandfather
2. What year did I get my patent?
   A. 1892
   B. 1890
   C. 1891
3. What did I do for a living?
   A. Beautician
   B. Dressmaker
   C. Teacher

Directions: Find the words associated with Sarah's life and career.

L	U	C	S	R	D	R	O	T	N	E	V	N	I	I	I	N	M	D
E	N	M	R	D	L	R	W	J	J	A	W	R	T	Y	I	B	D	D
F	D	I	C	A	G	U	E	C	Y	N	R	C	Q	S	R	G	K	P
Q	E	O	L	U	V	J	P	S	X	J	M	F	H	K	O	T	Q	Y
F	R	T	Z	L	D	E	Y	A	S	H	F	V	C	Y	N	C	X	L
Q	G	G	C	P	O	S	N	Q	K	M	G	K	Q	V	I	K	P	T
C	R	Z	U	O	D	S	A	C	K	X	A	Y	N	J	N	P	Q	H
W	O	F	H	Z	Q	Y	O	Y	O	W	J	K	L	M	G	J	T	F
Y	U	W	H	E	E	F	X	D	Q	U	N	Q	E	V	B	Y	T	P
E	N	H	O	S	L	K	Q	H	I	B	N	O	I	R	O	K	V	F
Y	D	P	S	G	N	D	K	I	M	T	J	T	K	Y	A	T	O	F
L	R	K	U	T	Z	E	A	K	J	J	G	F	Y	Q	R	X	A	D
P	A	V	L	A	N	H	W	U	M	F	K	M	I	V	D	F	R	B
S	I	P	O	T	R	E	T	H	B	C	R	A	W	L	I	V	I	C
F	L	S	V	P	Y	B	T	B	A	L	P	E	W	T	M	Z	L	K
Q	R	Y	K	O	K	W	E	A	A	V	R	P	B	D	Z	M	A	P
K	O	X	B	J	V	S	D	X	P	F	E	V	U	J	C	C	F	L
L	A	D	I	E	S	-	G	A	R	M	E	N	T	S	N	O	O	N
U	D	P	E	I	G	H	T	-	C	H	I	L	D	R	E	N	G	X

Find These Words

CRAVENCOUNTY
NEWHAVEN
PATENTS
IRONINGBOARD
LADIES-GARMENTS

INVENTOR
DRESSMAKER
CIVILWAR
UNDERGROUNDRAILROAD
EIGHT-CHILDREN

Directions: Read and answer the questions. These are your opinions so the answers will vary.

If you could meet a cartoon character in real life, who would you pick?

Who is a friend at school that you know you can count on?

What is one thing you want to know about your teacher?

Directions: Read and answer the questions below. There are clues in the puzzle to help you. Try and solve the cryptic message.

Clue for cryptic message: Sarah and this person have something in common.

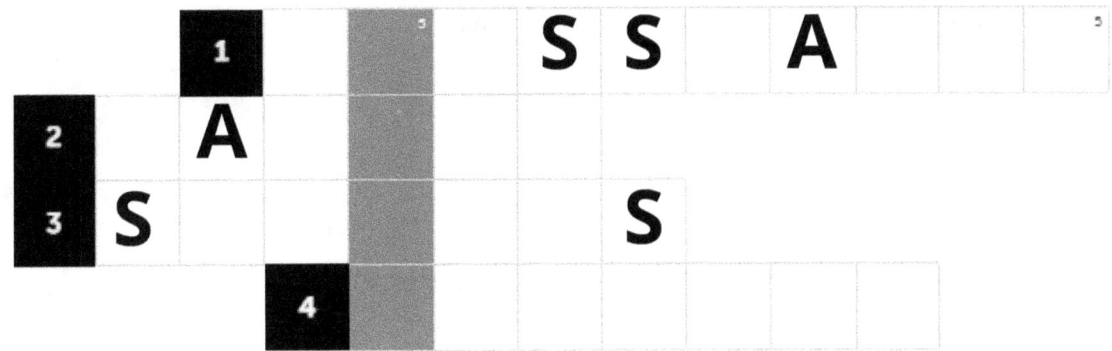

Questions

1) Sarah worked as a ____ in New Haven, CT.
2) Sarah was among the first black women in American history to receive a ____.
3) Sarah's ironing board was designed to improve the quality of ironing the ____ and bodies of women's garments.
4) Sarah belonged to the ____ Avenue Congregational Church.

Directions: This is the WGLT Challenge. Solve the cryptogram. As the puzzle solver, you need to find which number belongs to which character. And this can be pretty challenging! You will need to match the number with the letter. There are some letters given to you below. This will help you solve the other words and unlock more characters. **Good Luck.**

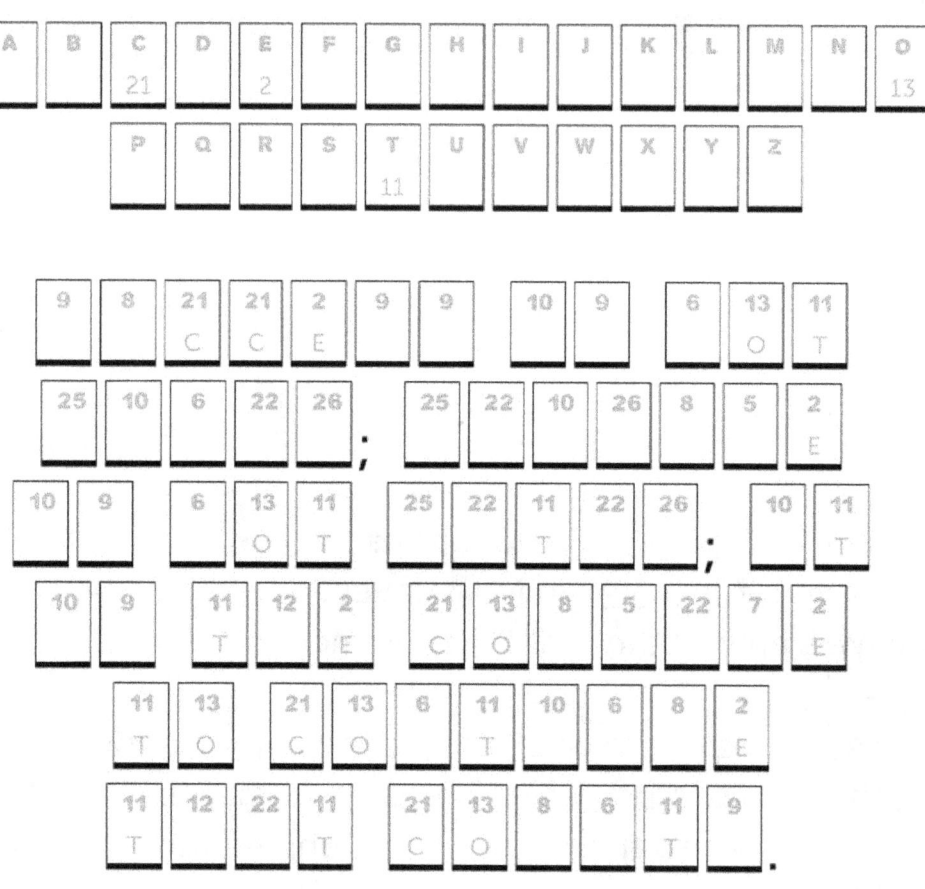

Lyda D. Newman

Lyda D. Newman

**1885 – UNKOWN
HAIRDRESSER**

LEFT BLANK ON PURPOSE

Lyda D. Newman

Lyda D. Newman

Lyda D. Newman

Lyda D. Newman

Lyda D. Newman

Lyda D. Newman

Directions: read the bio below and answer the following questions.

Hi, my name is Lyda D. Newman. I was born in 1885 in Ohio. I worked as a hairdresser in various New York City directories, as well as Newport, RI, during the summer time. While doing hair, I noticed how hard it was to effectively style textured hair with brushes made from animal hair. In 1898, I made improved the hairbrush by using synthetic bristles instead of the animal hairs that were commonly used for brushes at the time. My changes made hairbrushes more durable. This type of brush could also be taken apart easily for cleaning because it contained a compartment at the bottom that could be removed from the back and cleaned. All you had to do was hit a button that, when clicked, would detach the bristle part and allow a new one to be put in. This meant that hairdressers could now have a new brush instead of having to clean the brush between clients.

1. Where did I go to do hair in the summer time?
   A. New York City
   B. Newport
   C. Harlem
2. What did I do for a living?
   A. Hairdresser
   B. Public Speaker
   C. Maid
3. I made an improvement to what invention?
   A. Curling Irons
   B. Clippers
   C. Hairbrush

Directions: Answer the questions, to solve the crossword puzzle. You can use the internet if you get stuck on any question.

Across

1) Lyda spent her time _____ neighborhoods in New York City to educate them on things like voting rights.
4) Lyda design was specifically made for ____ hair.
5) Lyda's brush was also unique because it had an _____ that allowed airflow to the bristles, which helped the brush dry much faster.
6) Lyda's primary occupation was hair care as she listed "_____."
7) Lyda fought to give women the legal right to ____.

Down

2) Lyda was an active member and organizer for the women's _____ movement.
3) Lyda is known for the invention of a durable hairbrush with ____ bristles.
4) Lyda hair brush had synthetic bristles instead of ____ hair.

Directions: Read and answer the questions. These are your opinions so the answers will vary.

If you could meet one celebrity, who would it be?

What is something that you are thankful for?

What is a family tradition that you have?

Directions: Unscramble the words below about Lyda. See if you can get the bonus word.

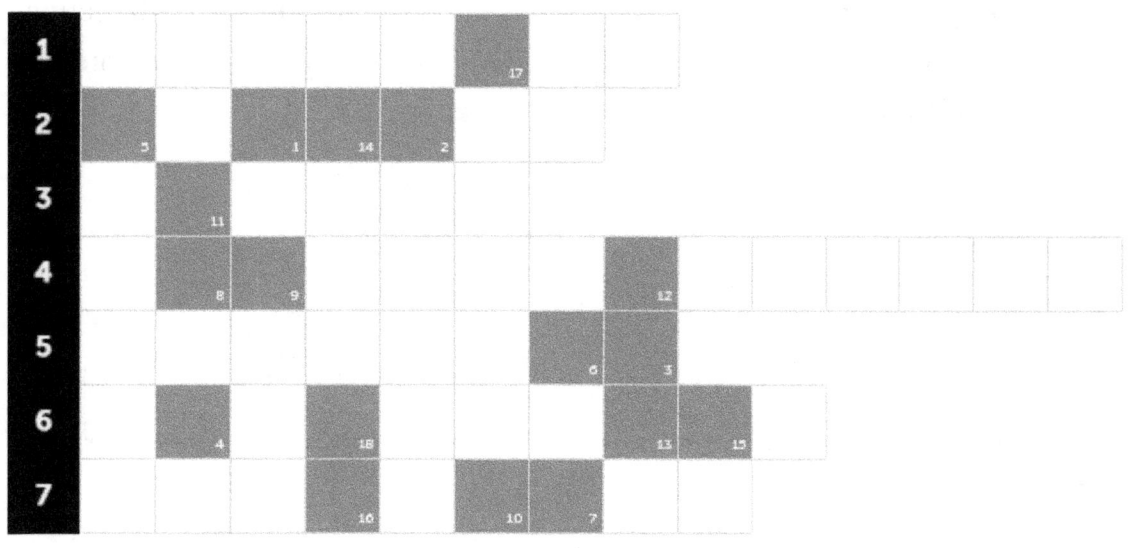

BONUS WORD

Unscramble Words

1) vneonrti
2) wreptno
3) eptnat
4) oazilfteactefg
5) iimctasv
6) 2yaaelsnec
7) ruhbshira

Directions: This is the WGLT Challenge. Solve the cryptogram. As the puzzle solver, you need to find which number belongs to which character. And this can be pretty challenging! You will need to match the number with the letter. There are some letters given to you below. This will help you solve the other words and unlock more characters. **Good Luck.**

1. What was the name of the restaurant I got my start at?
   A. Crum's
   B. Moon Lake House
   C. Knickerbocker Hall Restaurant
2. What year did I open Crum's?
   A. 1850
   B. 1855
   C. 1860
3. I'm known as the person who invented?
   A. Potato Chips
   B. Fine cuisine
   C. Fried wild duck

George Speck
Answers

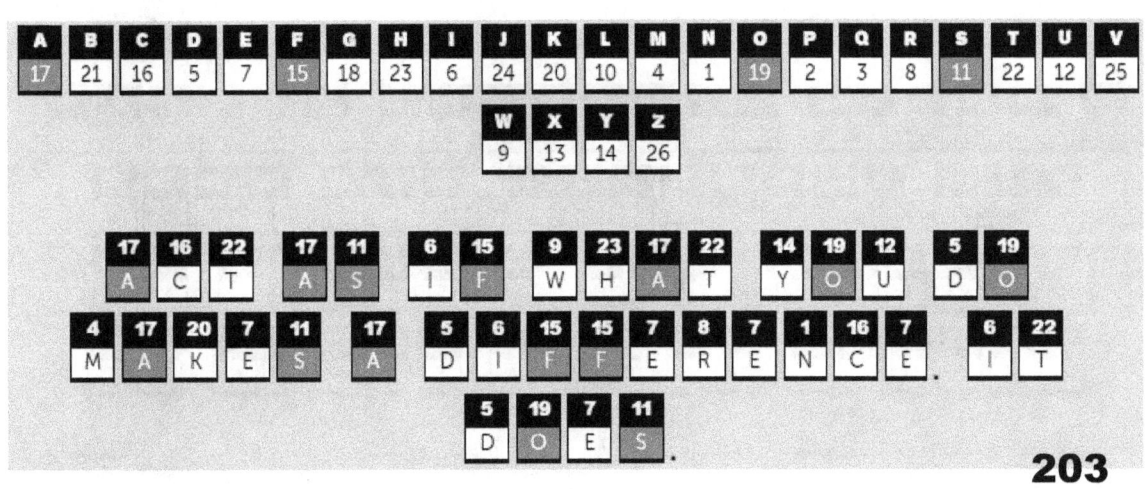

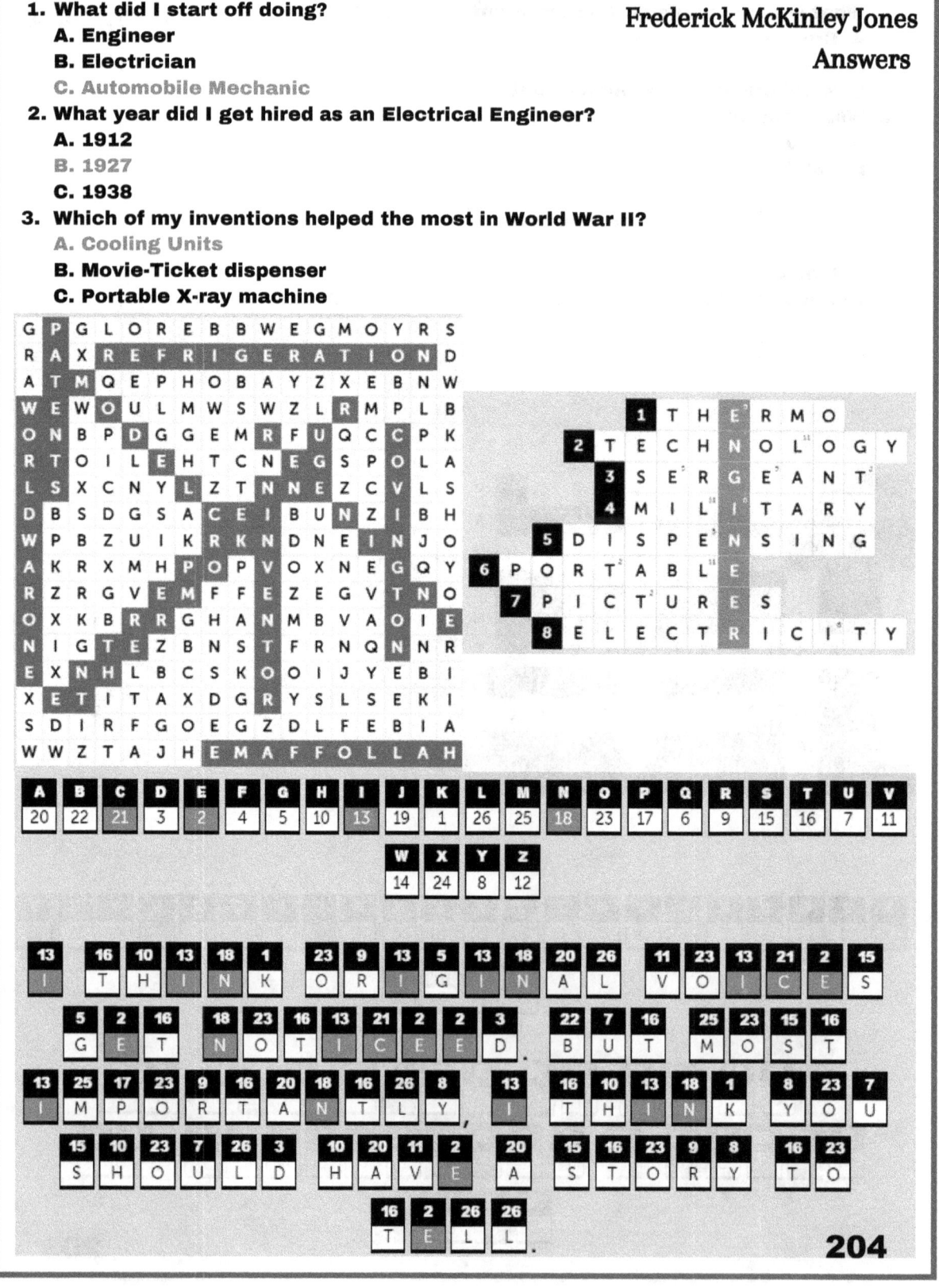

Garrett Morgan Answers

1. What was considered my first invention?
   A. Improved sewing machine
   B. Zigzag attachment
   C. Breathing device
2. What year did I open my own business?
   A. 1908
   B. 1907
   C. 1906
3. Which invention did I enhance with my idea?
   A. Chemical hair-processing
   B. Smoke hood
   C. Traffic signal

IF YOU WANT TO DO SOMETHING THEN BE THE BEST.

205

Marie Van Brittan Brown
Answers

1. What was my profession before my invention?
   A. Electrician
   B. Nurse
   C. Security
2. What year did I get my patent for my invention?
   A. 1966
   B. 1969
   C. 1960
3. What did I invent to make me feel more safe?
   A. Door Lock
   B. Peep hole
   C. Security System

Crossword:
1. CREDITED
2. SCIENCE
3. INSPIRED
4. COMMUNICATION
5. INVENTED
6. DAUGHTER
7. SYSTEM
8. PEEPHOLES
9. THIRTEEN

A	B	C	D	E	F	G	H	I	J	K	L	M	N	O	P	Q	R	S	T	U	V
18	7	3	6	22	8	4	12	11	26	9	13	16	5	17	19	2	25	10	15	20	21

W	X	Y	Z
23	1	24	14

"WE MUST BELIEVE THAT WE ARE GIFTED FOR SOMETHING AND THAT THIS MUST BE ATTAINED."

206

George Washington Carver Answers

1. Where did I get my Masters degree from?
   A. Highland University
   B. Iowa State University
   C. Simpson College
2. What fraternity am I a member of?
   A. Phi Beta Sigma
   B. Alpha Phi Alpha
   C. Omega Phi Psi
3. What product didn't I develop?
   A. Milk
   B. Peanut Butter
   C. Soap

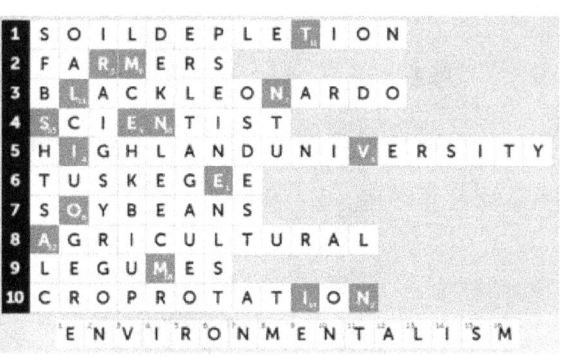
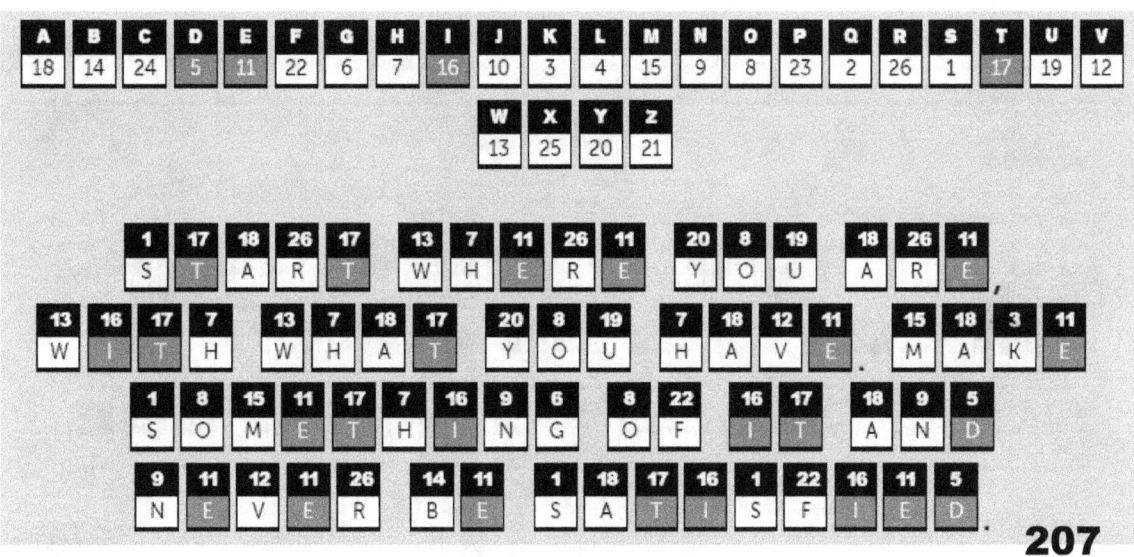

"START WHERE YOU ARE, WITH WHAT YOU HAVE. MAKE SOMETHING OF IT AND NEVER BE SATISFIED."

207

Granville Woods Answers

1. What was not one of the skills I learned when I was 10?
   A. Electrician
   B. Machinist
   C. Blacksmith
2. What year did I get my first patent?
   A. 1885
   B. 1884
   C. 1887
3. Which patent did I sell to American Bell?
   A. Telegraphony
   B. Steam boiler
   C. Synchronous Multiplex Railway Telegraph

Word search solutions include: AIRBRAKE, TELEGRAPH, PATENTS, BEAM, GENERAL ELECTRIC, STREETCARS, EDISON, CINCINNATI

Crossword:
1. ELECTRIC
2. BOILER
3. TELEGRAPHONY
4. MULTIPLEX
5. CINCINNATI
6. EDISON

Cipher key:
A=24, B=18, C=16, D=3, E=7, F=17, G=8, H=2, I=23, J=1, K=6, L=25, M=26, N=5, O=4, P=15, Q=10, R=14, S=9, T=11, U=19, V=20, W=13, X=22, Y=12, Z=21

"IF A CHILD CANNOT LEARN IN THE WAY WE TEACH, WE MUST TEACH IN A WAY THE CHILD CAN LEARN."

208

1. What college did I get my Masters degree from?
   A. University of Alabama
   B. Tuskegee University
   C. Fisk University
2. Who did I go to work for in 1979?
   A. U.S. Airforce
   B. NASA
   C. Tuskegee University
3. In 1991 I partnered with Hasbro to sell?
   A. Nerf Gun
   B. Super Soaker
   C. Toy Robots

Lonnie Johnson
Answers

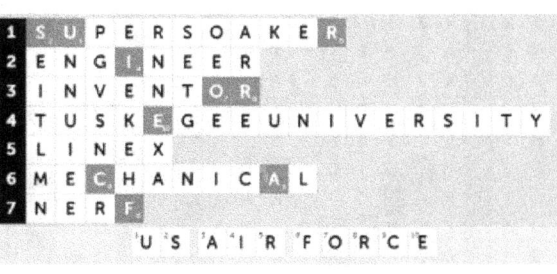
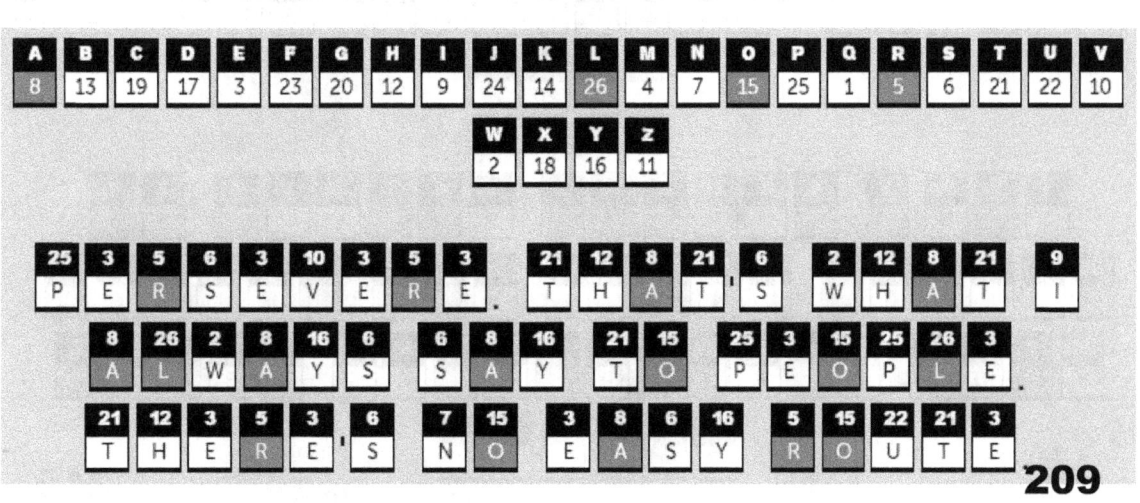

"PERSEVERE. THAT'S WHAT I ALWAYS SAY TO PEOPLE. THERE'S NO EASY ROUTE"

1. Where did I get my Bachelors degree from?
   A. New York University
   B. New York City College of Technology
   C. Brown University
2. What job allowed me to invent software to create GIFs?
   A. BET
   B. Macromedia
   C. The White House
3. What is the name of the company I founded?
   A. The FeedRoom
   B. tEquitable
   C. Taligent

Lisa Gelobter

Answers

Crossword:
1. FOUNDER
2. URBAN
3. DIGITAL
4. INCREMENTAL
5. EDUCATION

Cipher key:

A	B	C	D	E	F	G	H	I	J	K	L	M	N	O	P	Q	R	S	T	U	V
16	5	26	1	4	13	9	3	11	21	17	23	6	10	7	25	18	15	24	2	22	14

W	X	Y	Z
12	8	20	19

"DON'T EXPECT PEOPLE TO CHANGE UNTIL YOU CHANGE YOUR PERCEPTIONS ABOUT PEOPLE."

210

1. What college did I get my Masters degree from?
   A. Stanford University
   B. University of Tennessee
   C. Florida Atlantic University
2. What company did I work for?
   A. IBM
   B. Apple
   C. Microsoft
3. Which invention is not mine?
   A. ISA systems bus
   B. Personal Computer
   C. Gigahertz chip

Mark E. Dean

Answers

Crossword answers:
1. COMPUTERENGINEER
2. ISABUS
3. INVENTOR
4. PROCESSORCHIP
5. HALLOFFAME
6. NEWSANDWORLDREPORT
7. ONEGIGAHERTZ

IBM FELLOW

Down/across answers: INVENTORS, ENGINEERS, PROFESSOR, ENGINEERING, MIGRAHER(?), ELECTRICAL, THREE, COLOR(?), MDMS(?)

Cryptogram:
"A LOT OF KIDS GROWING UP TODAY AREN'T TOLD THAT YOU CAN BE WHATEVER YOU WANT TO BE. THERE MAY BE OBSTACLES, BUT THERE ARE NO LIMITS."

Percy Lavon Julian
Answers

1. What college did I get my Ph. D from?
   A. DePauw University
   B. University of Vienna
   C. Harvard University
2. What honor society do I belong to?
   A. Phi Kappa Phi
   B. Gamma Beta Phi
   C. Phi Beta Kappa
3. Chemical synthesis of medicinal drugs helps treat?
   A. Arthritis
   B. Open wounds
   C. Headache

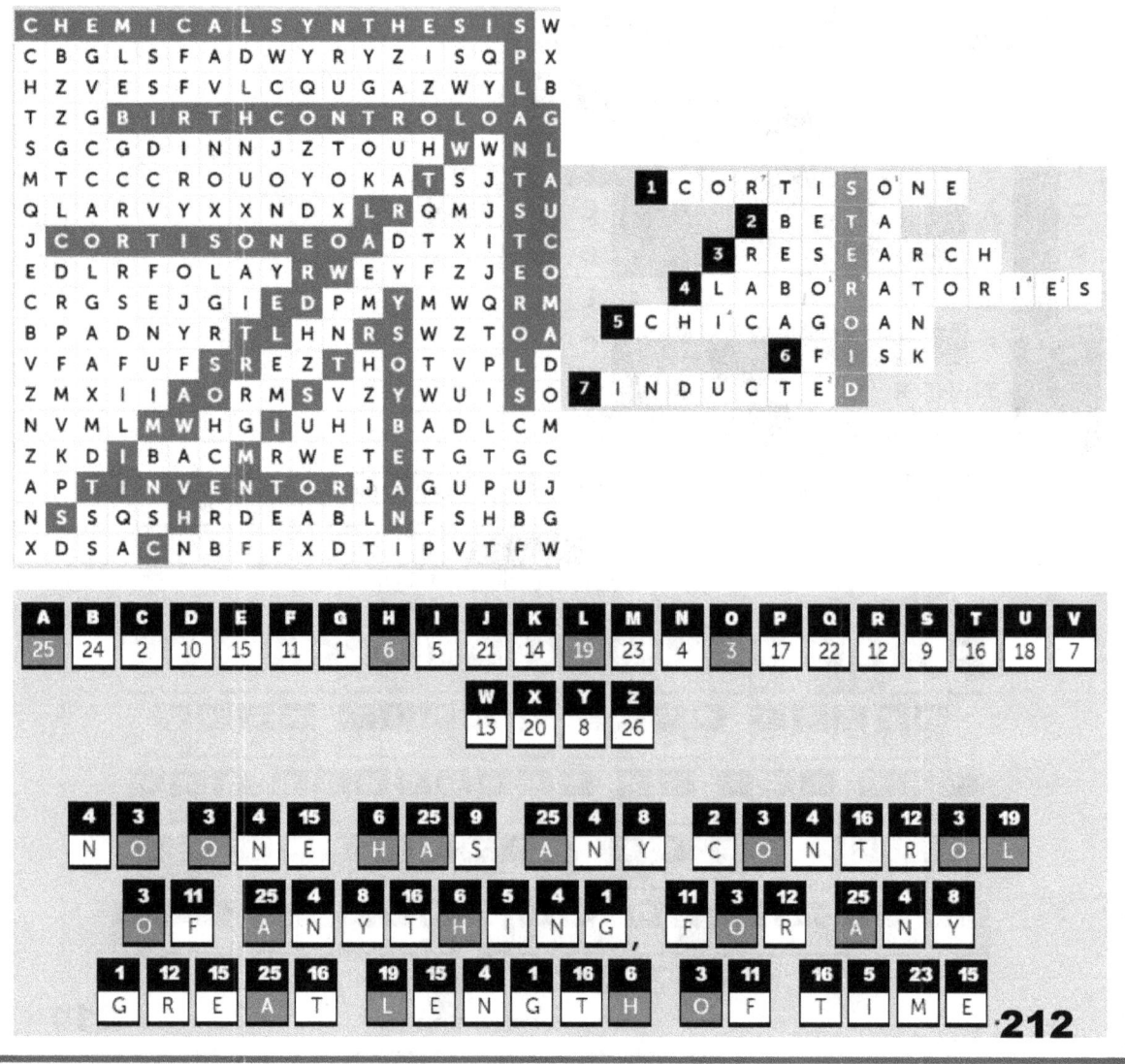

NO ONE HAS ANY CONTROL OF ANYTHING, FOR ANY GREAT LENGTH OF TIME

Otis Boykin
Answers

1. What HBCU did I go to?
   A. Clark University
   B. Fisk University
   C. Morehouse College
2. What year did I get my first patent?
   A. 1959
   B. 1961
   C. 1946
3. Electrical resistors aren't used in?
   A. Guided missiles
   B. Pacemakers
   C. Watch

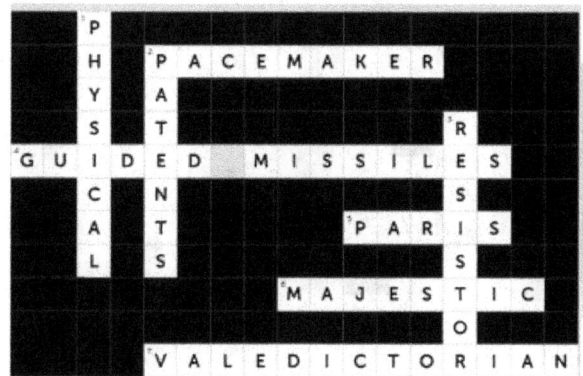
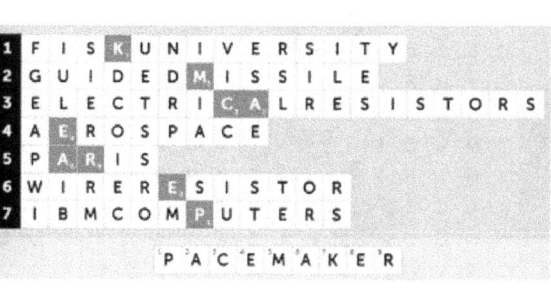

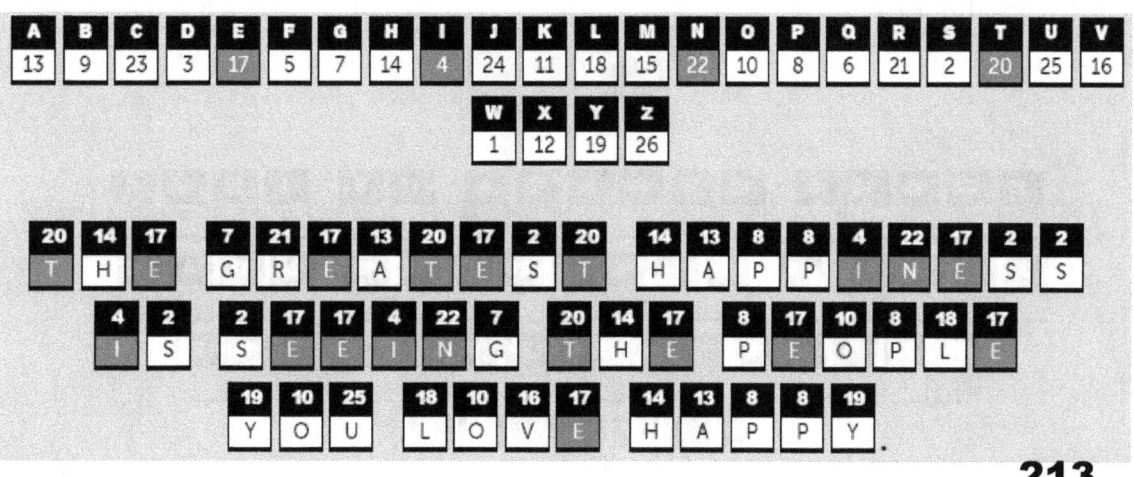

"THE GREATEST HAPPINESS IS SEEING THE PEOPLE YOU LOVE HAPPY."

213

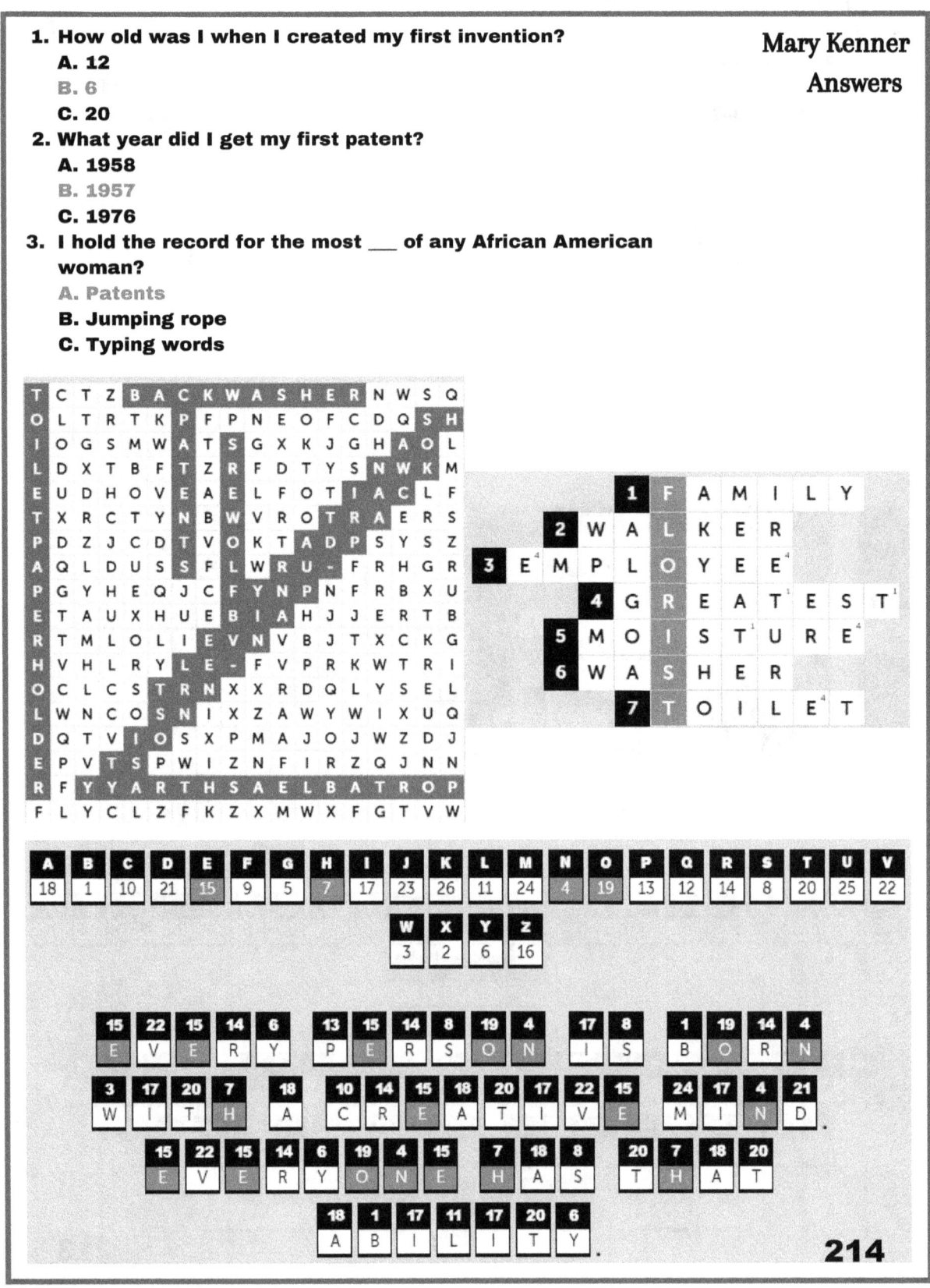

Philip Downing

Answers

1. What did I do for work for over thirty years?
   A. Postal Master
   B. Postal Clerk
   C. Postal Driver
2. What year did I get my second patent?
   A. 1891
   B. 1890
   C. 1917
3. Which patent didn't have to do with the Post Office?
   A. Envelope moistener
   B. Mail box
   C. Electrical switch

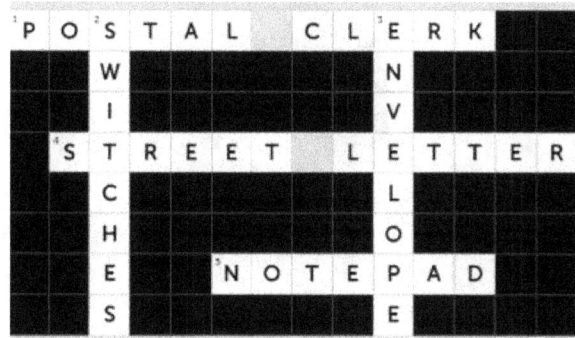
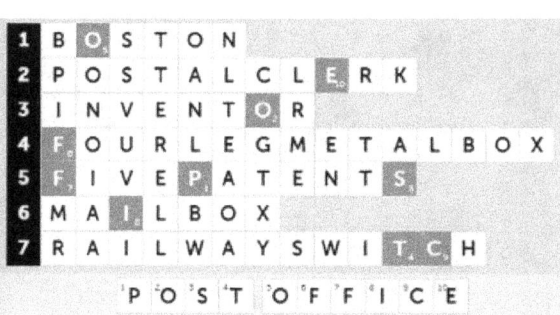
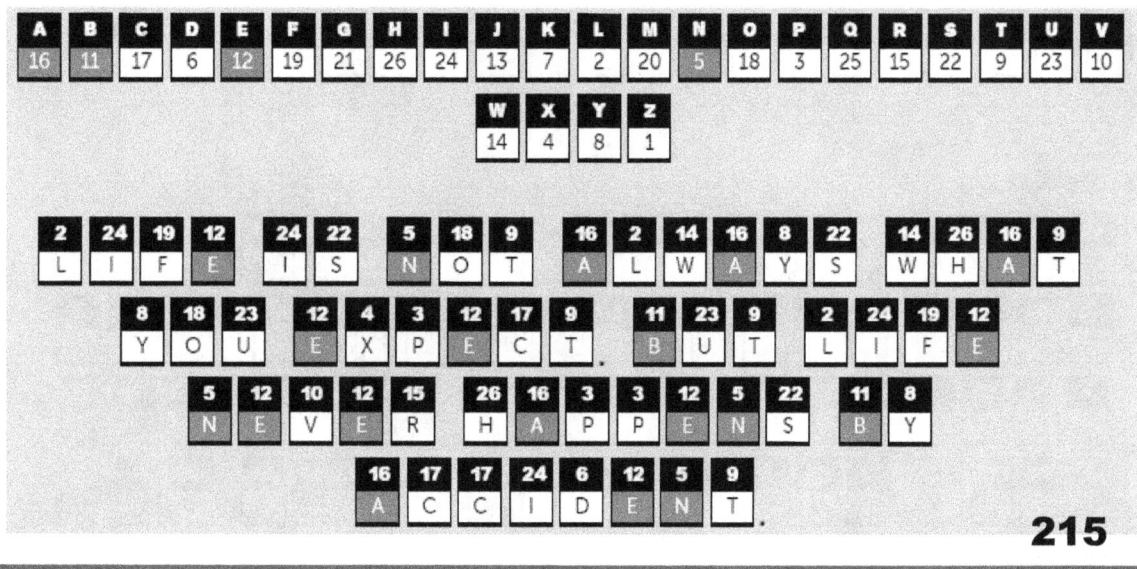

LIFE IS NOT ALWAYS WHAT YOU EXPECT. BUT LIFE NEVER HAPPENS BY ACCIDENT.

215

Lewis Latimer Answers

1. What war did I serve in?
   A. World War I
   B. Civil War
   C. World War II
2. Which invention of mine helped improve the light bulb?
   A. Water Closet for Railroad Cars
   B. Electric Lamp
   C. Process of Manufacturing Carbons
3. What ship did I serve on in the U.S. Navy?
   A. USS Massasoit
   B. USS Galena
   C. USS Monitor

Crossword:
1. EDISON
2. CROSBY
3. NAVY
4. FILAMENTS
5. EIGHT
6. HISTORIC
7. BATHROOM
8. MECHANICAL
9. CONDITIONING

Cipher:
"WE CREATE OUR FUTURE, BY WELL IMPROVING PRESENT OPPORTUNITIES; HOWEVER FEW AND SMALL THEY BE."

216

Henry T. Sampson
Answers

1. What fraternity am I a member of?
   A. Alpha Phi Alpha
   B. Omega Psi Phi
   C. Kappa Alpha Psi
2. What year did I get a patent for the gamma-electric cell?
   A. 1964
   B. 1973
   C. 1971
3. I was the first African American in the U.S. to what?
   A. Earn a PhD. in chemical engineering
   B. Earn a PhD. in music engineering
   C. Earn a PhD. in nuclear engineering

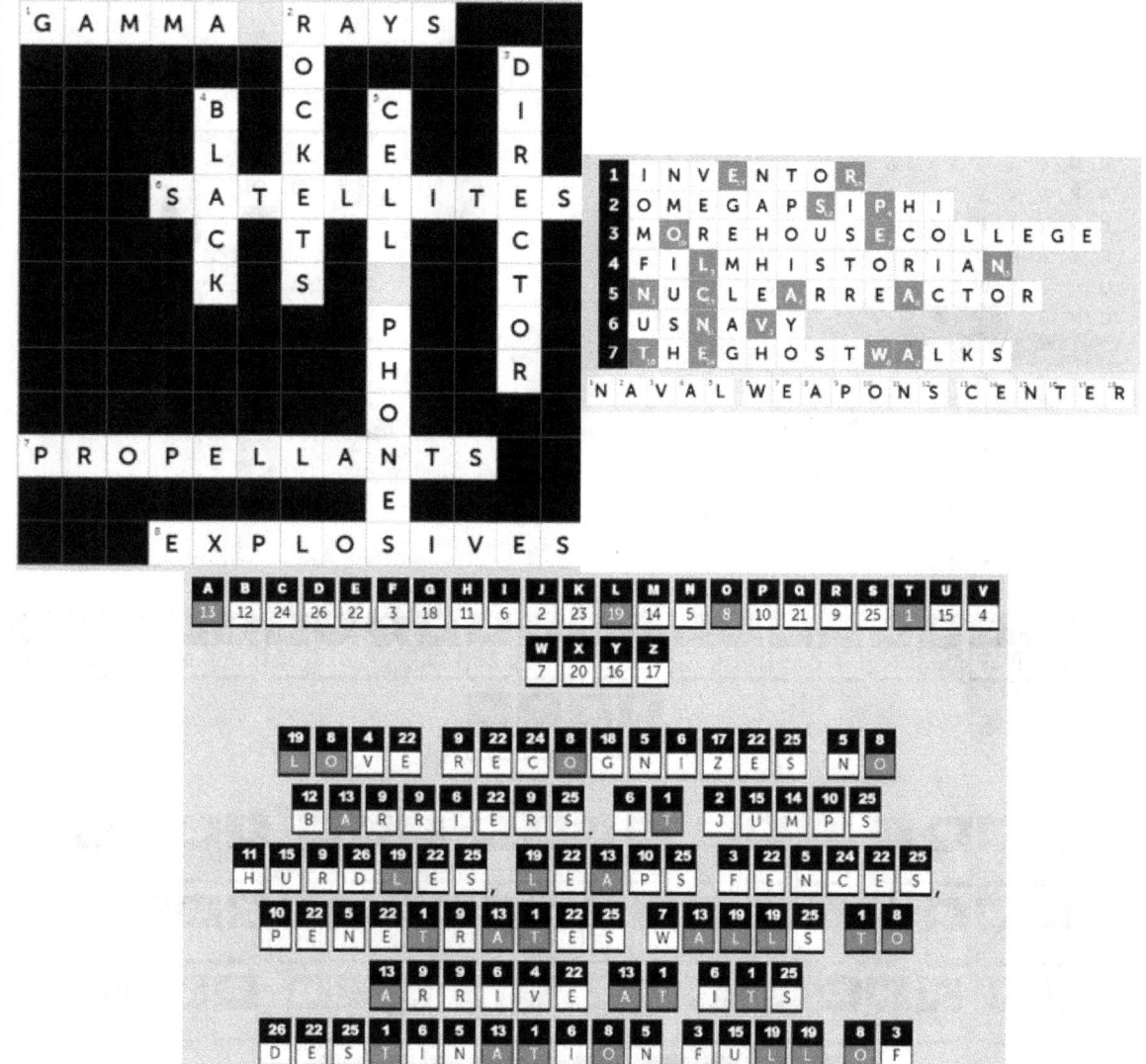

Sarah Breedlove Answers

1. Where did I learn about hair care?
   A. Annie Malone
   B. My Brothers
   C. My Parents
2. What year did I establish my base in Indianapolis?
   A. 1906
   B. 1908
   C. 1910
3. What made me want to learn about hair care?
   A. Severe dandruff
   B. My Daughters hair
   C. Baldness

Word search words: SHAMPOO, JAMAICA, POMADE, PETROLEUM JELLY, SOCIAL ACTIVIST, PITTSBURGH, IRON, PHILANTHROPY

Crossword:
1. SCALP
2. BUDGET
3. OLIVE
4. FREE
5. WASHERWOMAN
6. NAACP
7. BREEDLOVE
8. LELIA

Cipher key:
A	B	C	D	E	F	G	H	I	J	K	L	M	N	O	P	Q	R	S	T	U	V	W	X	Y	Z
22	5	13	26	12	3	25	11	20	16	2	7	23	18	14	6	15	19	21	17	10	9	8	24	4	1

"DON'T SIT DOWN AND WAIT FOR THE OPPORTUNITIES TO COME. GET UP AND MAKE THEM HAPPEN."

218

1. Where did I get certified as a mechanical engineer?
   A. University of Michigan
   B. Ontario Tech University
   C. University of Edinburgh
2. What year did I invent the automatic lubricator?
   A. 1872
   B. 1898
   C. 1899
3. What does the saying The real McCoy mean?
   A. Nickname
   B. Advertisement
   C. The real thing

Elijah J. McCoy
Answers

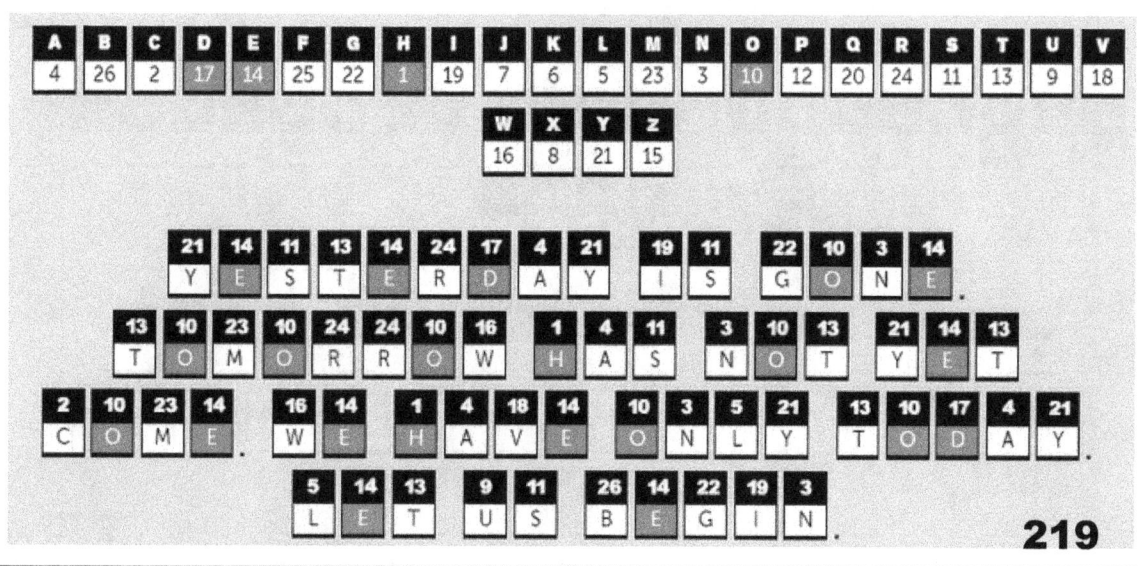

Alexander Miles
Answers

1. What did I do to make a living?
   A. Invent things
   B. Work in the Chamber of Commerce
   C. Barber
2. What year did I patent automatic elevator doors?
   A. 1881
   B. 1890
   C. 1887
3. What made me want to invent automatic elevator doors?
   A. Tired of closing them manually
   B. Make them easy to operate
   C. My daughter falling down the shaft

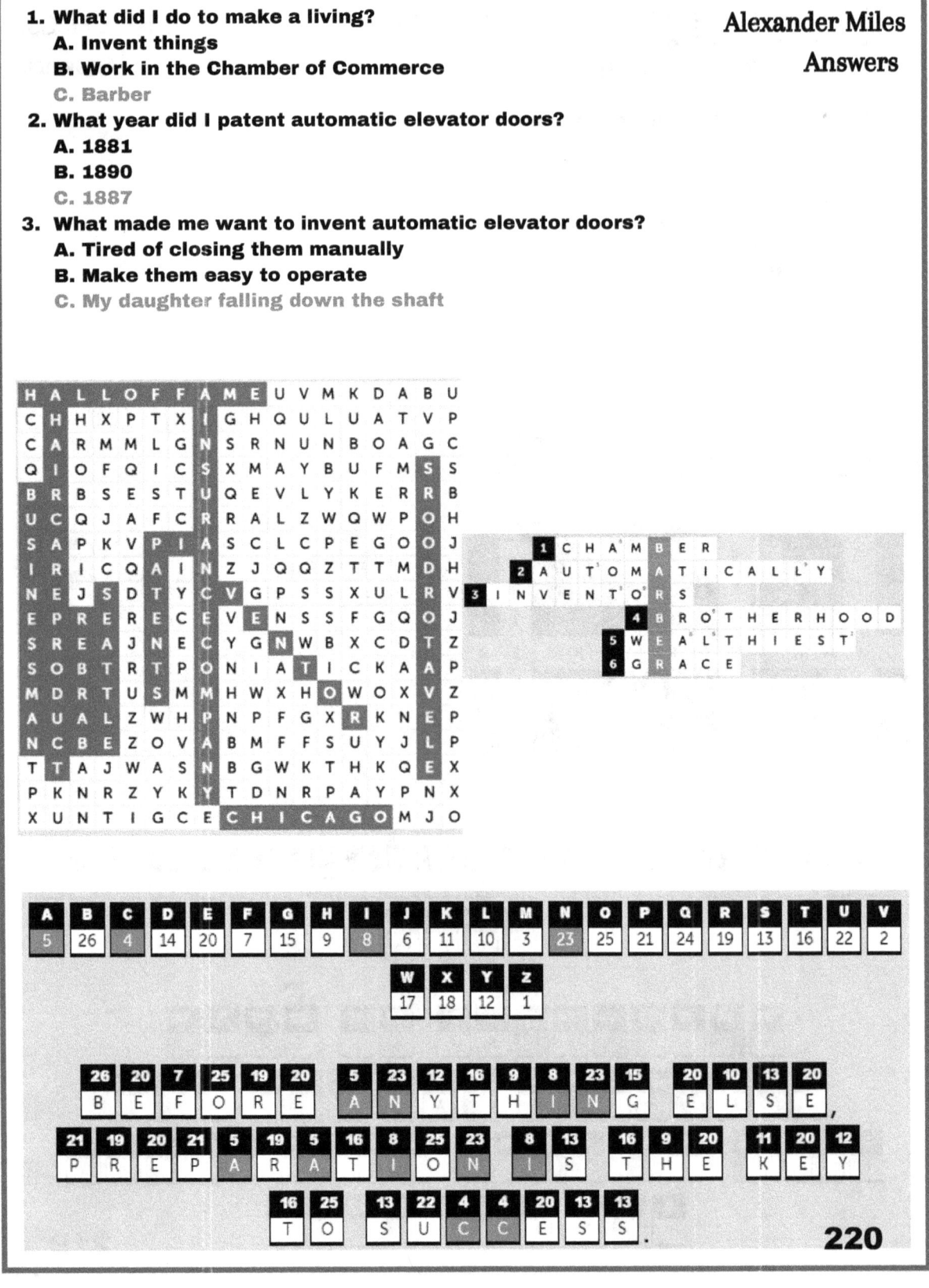

BEFORE ANYTHING ELSE, PREPARATION IS THE KEY TO SUCCESS.

Charles Drew
Answers

1. What college did I get my doctorate from?
   A. Amherst College
   B. Morgan College
   C. Columbia University
2. What year did I get patent for Preserving Blood?
   A. 1941
   B. 1942
   C. 1945
3. What HBCU was I a professor at?
   A. Fisk University
   B. Morgan College
   C. Morehouse College

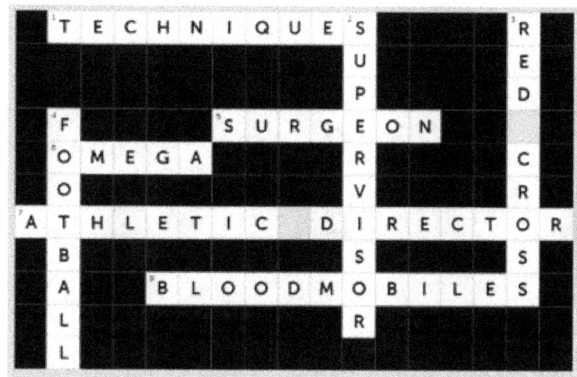

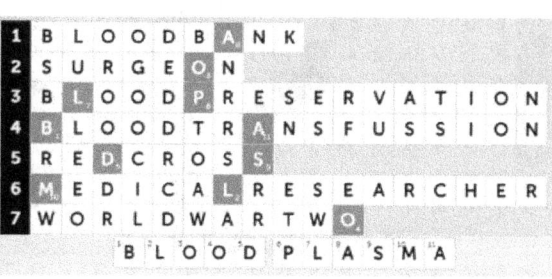

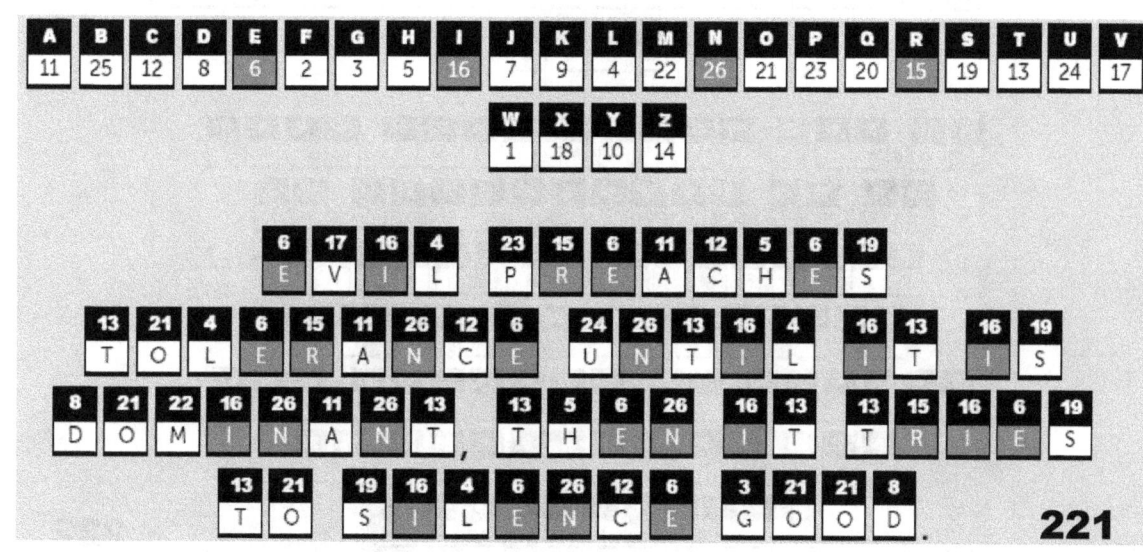

Patricia Bath
Answers

1. What college did I get my Bachelors degree from?
   A. Hunter College
   B. Howard University
   C. Columbia University
2. What year did I patent Laserphaco Probe?
   A. 1986
   B. 1988
   C. 1983
3. I was the first African American female in the U.S. to?
   A. Get my Ph.D in medicine
   B. Graduate from Howard University College of Medicine
   C. Receive a medical patent

Crossword:
1. OPHTHALMOLOGY
2. PREVENTION
3. WOMAN
4. ULTRASOUND
5. POST-GRADUATE
6. DOCTOR

"DO NOT ALLOW YOUR MIND TO BE IMPRISONED BY MAJORITY THINKING. REMEMBER THAT THE LIMITS OF SCIENCE ARE NOT THE LIMITS OF IMAGINATION."

Wallace Amos

Answers

1. **What branch of the service was I in?**
   A. Air Force
   B. Marine Corps
   C. Army
2. **What year did I open my first store?**
   A. 1980
   B. 1975
   C. 1970
3. **I'm the founder of what cookie?**
   A. Keebler Fudge Stripes
   B. Famous Amos chocolate-chip cookie
   C. Chips Ahoy chocolate-chip cookie

Crossword 1
- 1. ROCK N ROLL
- 2. NO
- 3. READ
- 4. AIRFORCE
- 5. MUFFIN
- 6. KA(KAUN)
- 7. TALLAHASSEE
- 8. GREAT COOKIE
- NAME / AMEE

Crossword 2
1. CHOCOLATE CHIP
2. COOKIES
3. US AIR FORCE
4. SIMON & GARFUNKEL
5. LEARN TO READ
6. LATKAS COOKIES
7. FAMOUS AMOS

TALENT AGENT

Cipher Key

A	B	C	D	E	F	G	H	I	J	K	L	M	N	O	P	Q	R	S	T	U	V
4	14	22	20	25	8	23	16	26	9	2	6	17	11	5	12	19	18	24	1	10	21

W	X	Y	Z
13	15	7	3

Quote

"THE THING IS NOT TO LEAVE UNFINISHED BUSINESS: MAKE EVERY DAY COUNT."

223

Marjorie Stewart Answers

1. Which HBCU did I graduate from?
   A. Spelman College
   B. Fisk University
   C. Bethune-Cookman College
2. What did I invent in 1928?
   A. Curling Iron
   B. Permanent wave machine
   C. Hot comb
3. What did myself and Mary McLeod Bethune found?
   A. NAACP
   B. United Barbers Assoc
   C. United Beauty School Owners and Teachers Assoc

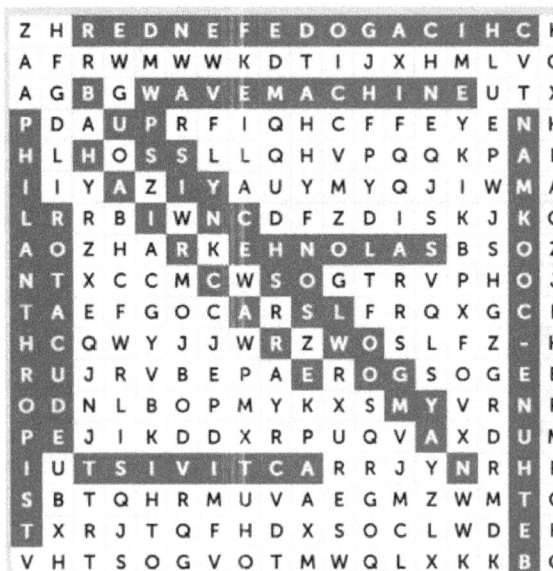

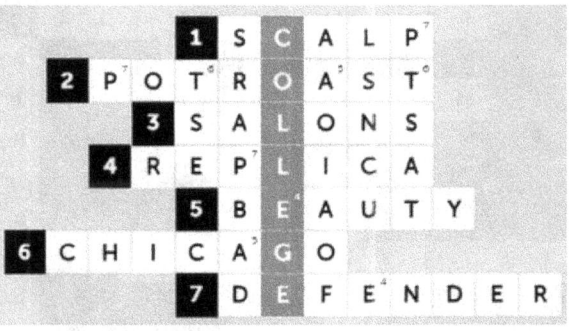

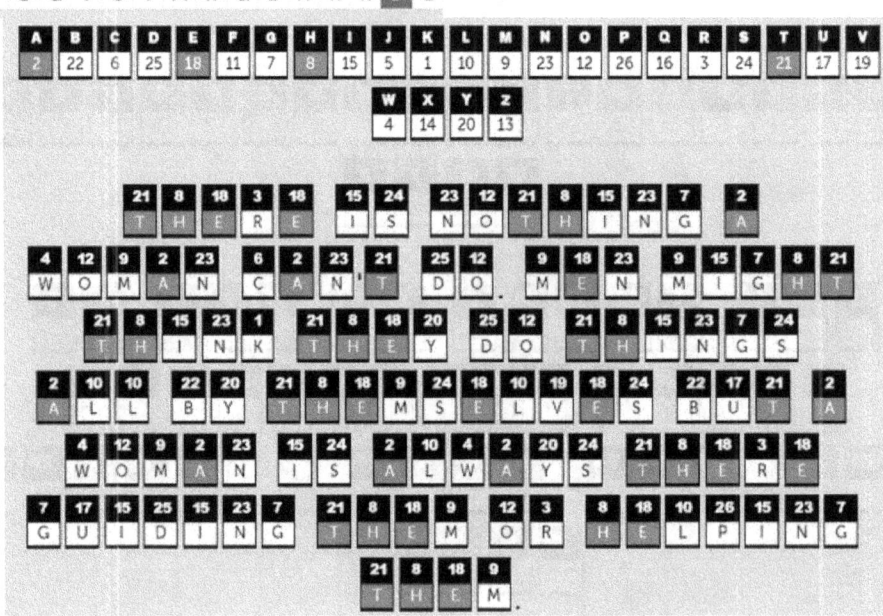

"THERE IS NOTHING A WOMAN CAN'T DO. MEN MIGHT THINK THEY DO THINGS ALL BY THEMSELVES BUT A WOMAN IS ALWAYS THERE GUIDING THEM OR HELPING THEM."

224

Gerald Lawson
Answers

1. What college didn't I go to?
   A. Queens College
   B. New York University
   C. City College of New York
2. What is the name of the arcade game I created?
   A. Pac Man
   B. Frogger
   C. Demolition Derby
3. What is my nickname?
   A. Father of microprocessors
   B. Father of the videogame cartridge
   C. Father of the coin arcade

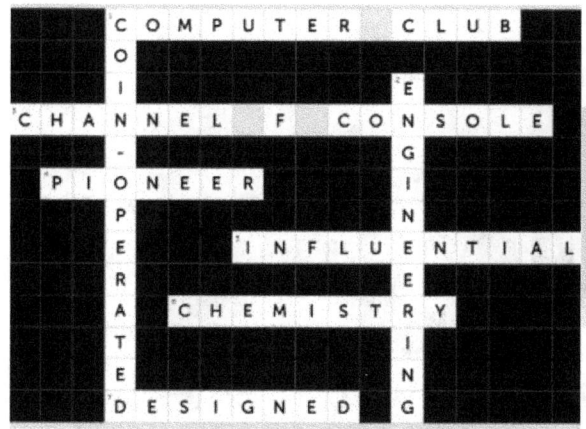
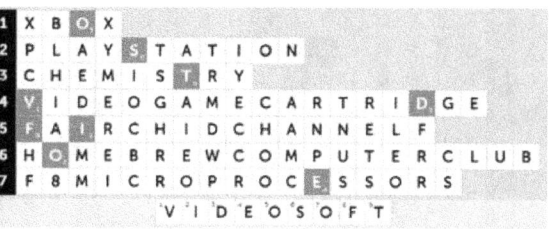
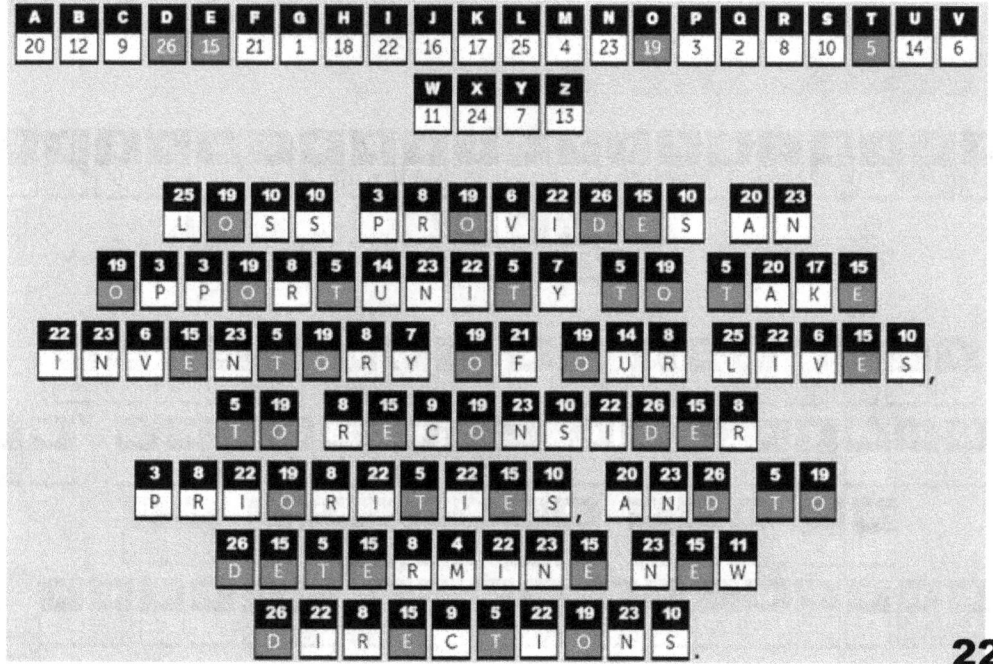

1. Who did I receive my education from?
   A. High School Teacher
   B. Grandmother
   C. Grandfather
2. What year did I get my patent?
   A. 1892
   B. 1890
   C. 1891
3. What did I do for a living?
   A. Beautician
   B. Dressmaker
   C. Teacher

Sarah Marshall

Answers

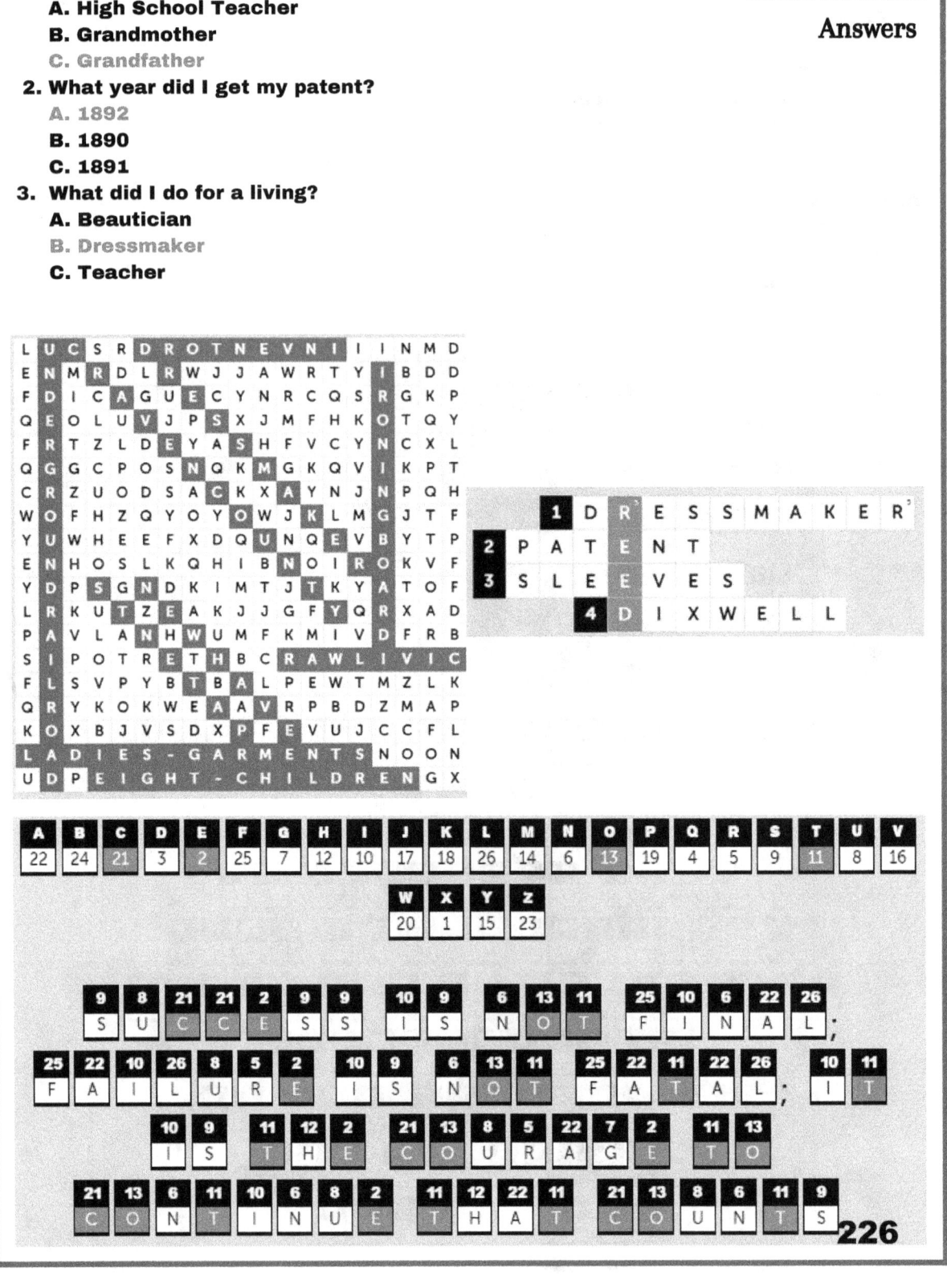

226

1. Where did I go to do hair in the summer time?
   A. New York City
   B. Newport
   C. Harlem
2. What did I do for a living?
   A. Hairdresser
   B. Public Speaker
   C. Maid
3. I made an improvement to what invention?
   A. Curling Irons
   B. Clippers
   C. Hairbrush

Lyda D. Newman
Answers

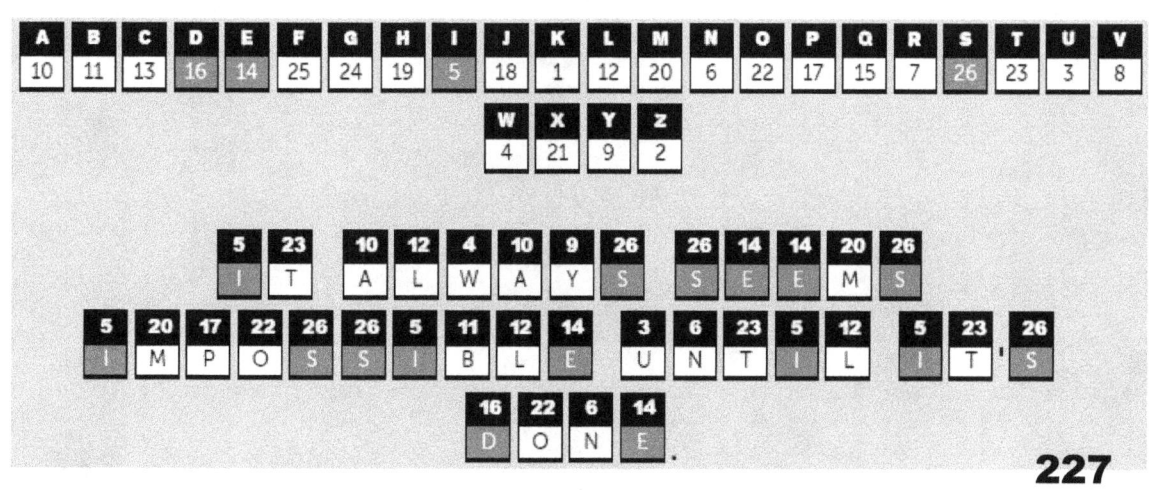

This book is dedicated to my grandkids
Anais Isabella Pablo-Antonio
Deyshawn Frank Chambers
Alicia Marie Jackson
Ayianna Marie Chambers
Zion Jamaris Jackson
Jayvon Jerome Jackson

ABOUT THE AUTHOR

Matthew D. Hale, the author of Black Historical Figures is a retired Marine and disabled veteran. He received his Bachelor of Arts in Computer Science from Campbell University and his Master of Science in Computer Engineering from Boston University. Matthew spends his down time making music, traveling, playing, and developing his own video games. Follow Matthew on Facebook/Meta at wegonnalearntoday, Instagram @ w_g_l_t and Tic Tok at wegonnalearntoday. Go to wegonnalearntoday.com or everydollarcountz.com for additional information.

In 2020 Matthew developed an interactive website, www.wegonnalearntoday, to provide access to Black History through games, music and videos. The website grew into the Black Historical Figures workbook series as a way to supplement the black history curricula taught in the school systems.

10 BOOK SERIES
RELEASE DATES

NOVEMBER 2022

FEBRUARY 2023

MAY 2023

AUGUST 2023

NOVEMBER 2023

GET YOUR COPY TODAY
DON'T FORGET TO TELL A FRIEND

www.ingramcontent.com/pod-product-compliance
Lightning Source LLC
Chambersburg PA
CBHW080335170426
43194CB00014B/2570